Growing
Your Soul

Growing Your Soul

Practical Steps to Increase Your Spirituality

Neil B. Wiseman

Fleming H. Revell
A Division of Baker Book House Co
Grand Rapids, Michigan 49516

A FORMER PASTOR and magazine editor, Neil Wiseman now serves as professor of pastoral development at Nazarene Bible College in Colorado Springs, Colorado.
AS A SEEKER after God, he invites his readers to look over his shoulder and into his heart as he strives to live an authentic life of devotion.

©1996 by Neil B. Wiseman

This book is based on *Spirituality: God's RX for Stress*, published by Beacon Hill Press, 1992.

Published by Fleming H. Revell
a division of Baker Book House Company
P.O. Box 6287, Grand Rapids, MI 49516-6287

Cover Design: The Puckett Group

Printed in the United States of America

Library of Congress Cataloging-in-Publication Data

Wiseman, Neil B.
    Growing your soul: practical steps to increase your spirituality / Neil B. Wiseman.
        p.   cm.
    Includes bibliographical references.
    ISBN 0-913367-59-1
      1. Spiritual life—Christianity. I. Title.
BV4501.2.W5742 1996
248.4—dc20   95-50276

Contents

Preface

The Starting Line

Empty lives, trying times, and shallow souls are no match for God. Never were. Not in Bible times. Not during the darkest centuries of human civilization or the most shameful years of church history. Not five hundred years ago. Not fifty years ago. Not now. And the dawning of the new century doesn't worry Him either. In matters of personal spiritual development, try to remember that the God who creates, rules, and holds the universe in His hands is the caring Father who loves you as if you were the only one to love. God wants the best for you. He's an incredible, selfless spendthrift when it comes to showering you with kindness, grace, and a second chance. God wants to walk with you every day, to wipe pain from your heart, and to fill your life with incredible gladness. God wants you home at His table. And He longs to celebrate your homecoming as did the prodigal's father.

Before you start reading *Growing Your Soul*, let's have a heart-to-heart talk. Growing a great soul is a pilgrimage with God where your innermost cravings for integration and holiness will be satisfied. Think of the glorious fulfillment inner wholeness can give you. Think of the full potential of discovering and living an authentic spirituality that enriches and directs life. Think of the meaning such intimacy with God provides. All these precious possibilities are transformed into realities as you grow a great soul.

Though some try to deny it, everyone has a built-in hunger for God. This yearning of the soul from the depths is as much a part of us as our hair color, shoe size, finger print, nose shape, or family history. This homesickness in the soul pursues us down every road we travel. Wherever we roam or however far we run, God keeps calling us home so we can be what He intended us to be when He made us.

Spirituality's substitutes never make good on their lofty promises—they never do because they can't. Think of all those unfulfilled people you know who have traveled down so many dead-end roads. Maybe you have had firsthand experience with some of these counterfeit substitutes. Education doesn't satisfy the deepest cravings. Money, security, sex, property, prominence, affluence, travel, and power all lack something. Government has let us down, so we feel overtaxed, cynical, and disillusioned. Religious legalism and superficial piety have proven to be shabby imitations of the real thing, so many who go to church regularly wonder why they do. Rationalism and secularism can't deliver either. All these collapsing substitutes, as interesting as they seemed at the start, tell us it's time to turn to God. The evening is fast approaching. It's time to start for home.

For years I counted too much on others to grow my soul. As a result of this dependence, my inner development was agonizingly slow and understandably shallow. Too many detours and side trips frustrated me. I counted too much on the lessons, sermons, self-help books, and inspirational songs of others. I expected too much from ministers, Sunday school teachers, writers, and singers. They all helped but not enough.

At the same time, I had another defeating presupposition. I mistakenly thought spirituality was confined to special places such as cathedrals, family camps, tabernacles, or the little church down the freeway. Somehow I thought growing my soul meant I had to be in some special holy place at some special time.

But the light broke like a spectacular sunrise in my soul when I discovered on an ordinary day that all of life is a portable sanctuary, to borrow Richard Foster's term.[1] That's when I finally realized that spirituality is not a lesson or a song or a place but a Person, a Presence, and an Intimacy. Spirituality, to be satisfying, requires paying close attention to God and watching the whole of life closely. It means sharpening our awareness, interaction, observation, and listening skills. It means exploring, questioning, receiving, and being transformed into the image of God's own dear Son.

My fuller way of growing a great soul helped me see that I live in the middle of a wealth of holy possibilities. If I let them, everyone I meet—children and the elderly and neighbors and students and secular columnists—can contribute something to my wholeness. Everywhere I go, someone or some event points me to my Friend, Teacher, Inner Monitor, and Sustainer.

This book invites you to use close-at-hand resources to develop your inner life. It describes many sacred delights and holy discoveries that are dressed in ordinary street clothes. It will help you be alert to many happy surprises all along this holy way. It shows you how to find so much delight in God that you will be willing to start again and sing and shout and laugh and pray and explore. Max Lucado describes this joyful journey so well: "It's what you always dreamed but never expected. It's the too-good-to-be true coming true. It's having God as your pinch-hitter, your lawyer, your dad, your biggest fan, and your best friend. God on your side, in your heart, out in front, and protecting your back. It's hope where you least expect it: a flower in life's sidewalk."[2]

Try growing a great soul for the sheer exhilaration of knowing God more fully. As you do you will become aware of an inner Companionship that sustains hope and supplies significance. Growing a great soul takes you back to the precious Source of everything that matters.

> **O the bliss of those**
> **who hunger and thirst**
> **for all that sets**
> **them right with God,**
> **for they shall be**
> **satisfied to the full.**
>
> *Matthew 5:6*
> *(Barclay)*

King of My Life and Lord of All

Oh, the incredible appetite I have for growing a great soul.

Today, I hunger for more of You. I seek You with my whole self—my mind, my will, and my emotions. In the midst of these confusing times, I long to know You better. I hunger for a holy life to make me spiritually whole and healthy. I am anxious to grow a great soul.

What
a worthwhile aim.
a glorious hope.
an adventuresome possibility.
an opportunity for partnership with You.

(Complete this prayer for yourself.)

To make it happen in my inner world,
    free me from . . .
Enable me to become . . .
And tear down every hindrance in me, such as . . .
I open my whole life to Your will and Your
    promise. Amen.

1

Hunger for the Holy

Finding Wholeness in Troubled Times

[We can keep ourselves so busy, fill our lives with so many diversions, stuff our heads with so much knowledge, involve ourselves with so many people and cover so much ground that we never have time to probe the fearful and wonderful world within.
—*John W. Gardner]*

"Is there anything more? What's missing?" A brilliant young Jewish law professor asked that probing question to a class as he concluded a guest lecture at Vanderbilt Divinity School.

His self-revelation shocked every student in the class: "I am a yuppie, tenured professor at Vandy with a life that sounds like the American dream. I have a beautiful wife and two bright kids. I live in a big house and own a BMW and a Cadillac. Even though I have everything any mother

13

ever wanted for her son, I am not happy. I thought you religion guys might have some answers. Is there something more?"

The professor's yearning describes the inner emptiness that money, possessions, and status never satisfy. Sadly, the Vandy students must have felt a similar void in their souls because no one attempted to answer the professor's question.

Like the law professor, tens of thousands inside and outside universities are famished for meaning. Some who feel this way live near us—in the next room or next door. Perhaps someone like that even lives in your skin and walks in your shoes. This hunger for the holy is described by author Judith C. Lechman as an "awful yawning emptiness created by God's absence."[1] Though contemporary people have many difficulties, more problems than we want to admit are rooted in spiritual incompleteness and inner God emptiness. From personal experience we know what emptiness and God's absence mean. Terms like boredom, purposelessness, lack of fulfillment, depression, emptiness, disillusionment, loss of values, and a hunger for the holy are complaints we often hear from others and sometimes use in reference to our own lives. When three-fourths of Americans believe the nation is in a serious moral and spiritual decline,[2] it's a good time to rekindle the enduring elements of spirituality, like courage, faith, love, and significance. It's time to find healing for what Albert Schweitzer once called a "sleeping sickness of the soul."

Moral Erosion Intensifies Our Hunger for the Holy

Moral erosion surrounds us everywhere in our contemporary world, causing the moral Richter scale to zoom through the roof. Dissatisfactions keep increasing. Violence mocks the Golden Rule. Rip-offs by petty thieves and corporation raiders have replaced business honesty. Children and women are abused or abandoned. Many young adults, raised without moral foundations or spiritual roots, lack spiritual strength to face even minor physical or emotional crises. Marriage vows are casually broken by divorce and infidelity. Meanwhile, the confidence of the elderly has been shaken by longer life that has less meaning.

In such a topsy-turvy world, many loud, so-called brilliant voices insist that they no longer believe in God. Their laughable logic insists they have outgrown Him. Such pseudo-sophistication shows they have either been duped by high-sounding nonsense or have never experienced vital faith. Others keep looking for newer, more intense sensations because their ordinary routines bore them. Meanwhile the occult, New Age, and old cults keep growing as people search for meaning and settle for counterfeit spirituality.

At the same time, a confusing inner tug-of-war—or is it a civil war?—pulls this generation between self-assertion and self-surrender. Many seem to work overtime to try to disprove the fact that the world cannot get along without moral foundations and spiritual underpinnings. But these efforts never work. Indeed, like arguing against gravity, their attempts only illustrate the necessity for eternal principles and holy guidance.

Anxiety always snowballs during periods of moral erosion like our present situation. For example, Karl Marx, Sigmund Freud, and their disciples indelibly imprinted their views on modern society. Though Marx and Freud both died mired in despair caused by their own conclusions, the aftershock and side effects of their theories continue to create tensions and undermine hope for millions to this day. Even a superficial comparison of our moral mess with the Ten Commandments helps us understand the fermenting anxieties many people feel these days.

Meanwhile, moral cancer cripples and kills individuals with shocking frustration and deadly consequences. Eroded values debilitate groups and weaken nations. When we face our contemporary situation candidly, we feel forced to agree with the former United Nations secretary, Dag Hammarskjöld: "You cannot play with the animal in you without becoming wholly animal, play with falsehood without forfeiting your right to truth, play with cruelty without losing your sensitivity of mind. He who wants to keep his garden tidy does not reserve a plot for weeds."[3]

Society, in this moral meltdown, is dizzied by crumbling absolutes and fatigued by the incredible pace. Fed-up people are crying out, "Where does all of this lead?" The obvious answer is "Nowhere." Nevertheless, we keep ourselves dazzled with accumulations and dizzy with incessant hurry that leads us down dead-end streets to empty nothingness. The frightening results should not surprise anyone. Our present dilemma is the predictable outcome of too little faith and too much activity and no moral foundations. Too often the problems are more inside us than in the world outside.

High-Tech Confusion Intensifies Our Hunger for the Holy

Technology has proven to be a blessing for many and a curse for others. Computers have revolutionized contemporary society at least as much as the printing press, electricity, or railroads reshaped earlier periods of human history. Modern weapons threaten nations and random shootings frighten individuals. Defense spending has nearly bankrupted the world. While calling it freedom of speech, the media, especially TV, has delivered smut, violence, and gloom into our living rooms and in the process corrupted our minds and infected our souls.

Birth control technology has changed sexual values, medicinal practices, family size, and school populations. Jet travel has made the world a global village and opened new business markets around the world. Smaller technological advances like supermarket scanners, microwave ovens, fax machines, phone-answering devices, and automatic teller machines have changed the way we think and work and spend money. VCRs have now shifted the entertainment habits of millions, for videos can be rented in thousands of places, including grocery stores and gas stations.

These changes cannot be undone, nor should we try. Who knows anyone who has ever won a war against technological progress? The dilemma is that technology has improved modern living at the same time that it has alarmingly decreased relationships, neighborhood contacts, church attendance, and quiet times with ourselves and God.

Spiritual poverty has become the black lung disease of the technical class. Consider what all this did to Mark Tighe, a thirty-one-year-old software programmer for Digital Equipment Corporation in Colorado Springs. Tighe's story shows the relationship between technology and moral emptiness. During the very early hours of a September morning, Tighe left his semi-rural Woodmoor home for a fifteen-minute drive to his workplace. When he arrived about 3:30 A.M., he logged in on his computer and composed a suicide note. After the printer typed his message, Mark taped the sheet to the wall. At 3:59 A.M., before shooting himself, he opened fire on a $200,000 computer system in what appeared to be a final statement of what technology did to him. Security guards discovered him dead near his computer keyboard at about

6:30 A.M. Later that morning, when they forced their way into Tighe's rustic house, police found his girlfriend's body. Apparently she had been murdered by a .45-caliber pistol that lay on the floor near the waterbed.[4]

Though investigating officers may never know all the facts in the Tighe case, this apparent suicide and murder illustrates the intensity of the emptiness and disconnectedness technology can cause. After allowing for emotional distress and severe fatigue, serious questions must be asked of a technical society that pushes people to the edge with corporate mergers, scientific wizardry, and high vocational demands. Mark's interest in life ran out because he drove himself too hard for too long in a technological jungle.

Clearly high tech stresses those involved in its design, manufacture, and distribution; but technophobia sometimes infects some who are forced to use it. Now that computers and other electronic devices have moved into most businesses and homes, there are those who fear the equipment: workers who feel undertrained and employees who have been automated out of a job. These high-tech changes put everyone on pins and needles.

Albert Einstein's sentence makes him sound like a prophet: "Technological progress is like an ax in the hands of a pathological criminal."

Good Life Seductions Intensify
Our Hunger for the Holy

"Seduced by the good life" is the way one high-placed industrial mogul describes our ferocious race to get things and our frightening loss of what really matters. Beyond the befuddling pressures like the expected need to sell oneself to a job, less-obvious deceivers lurk around every corner. All this is made worse by the fact we have too little time, too many choices, too few values, too many demands, and too few abiding commitments. Meanwhile, somewhere deep in the human spirit, a growing suspicion keeps reminding us that preoccupations with power, sex, busyness, and money have made the so-called good life lopsided. It's no wonder we feel "underwhelmed" by integrity, peace, and love.

[Actor Desmond Wilson] discussed the contradictions of the so-called good life with reporter Michael Dougan of the *San Francisco Examiner:* "I bought the American dream. I attained wealth and success and the world was an empty, desolate place for me." He continued: "My children didn't bring me any satisfaction. My wife didn't bring me joy. I didn't know how to love people; I tolerated them." Remembered for his role as Lamont in the TV comedy "Sanford and Son," Wilson went on to be Oscar in "The New Odd Couple." Raised in Harlem, he joked about his childhood: "My parents were in the iron and steel business—my mother ironed and my father stole." Though Wilson grew up the hard way, at the height of his acting career he owned a fleet of luxury cars, a twenty-seven-room Bel Air mansion, and everything that goes with such affluence. Still he was dissatisfied. His possessions owned him.[5] [His conclusion keeps repeating itself in too many lives—fast-lane living costs too much and pays too little.]

A brilliant senior from a prestigious eastern university reached the same judgment through a different series of circumstances. Before leaving for his overseas Peace Corps assignment, a Fortune 500 corporation recruiter offered him a fabulous, high-paying position. The recruiter, using what he considered his most convincing argument, told the graduating senior, "If you abandon the Peace Corps and work for us, you will become rich." The student, energized by his own search for meaning, answered with a compelling question, "What's the big deal about having lots of money?"

Anyone who chases money must eventually answer that question for himself or herself.

Greed, a near universal vice, fools us into behaving strangely. The modern saint George MacDonald exposed this tricky snare: "If it be *things* that slay you, what matter whether things you have, or things you have not?"[6] All this insatiable grasping wrecks relationships, stresses the heart, and sears the soul. As a result, the good life easily turns into a hellish merry-go-round that never stops. Greed always wants more—a lot more.

Chasing the good life often mocks high achievers too. Though big breaks and best salaries are promised in our society to the most talented, unusual ability sometimes causes seething jealousy in the workplace. Mediocre fellow employees resent the achiever, so threatened co-workers or tyrannical supervisors sometimes enjoy keeping gifted people in dead-end vocational slots. Sadly, destructive results follow for everyone: talented workers feel like overly controlled pawns, the enterprise they represent is weakened, and manipulating decision-makers die by inches when they think about their actions.

Fast-lane living, with the satisfaction that it promises but can't deliver, adds to the confusion. Epictetus, the ancient Greek, once observed correctly, "Man is disturbed not by things but by his ideas about things." He is right—stuff, securities, and status con us and lie to us.

However, an additional life-enriching issue must be factored into all these misdirected quests for life in the fast lane. Wherever any good life promises to lead us, however attractive or interesting, it is incomplete without Christ. A person who has everything but Christ will always be a pauper; therefore those who desire the authentic good life must include Jesus in their plans. To have everything but Christ produces the most frustrating kind of poverty; those who have nothing but Christ possess everything that matters. When God-denying lifestyles top the highest mountain of security and sophistication, they always find that spirituality and faith are what really satisfy.

Ceaseless Motion Intensifies Our Hunger for the Holy

⌈Too many daily activities overload our emotional circuits. Most of the time, we feel as if the whole world is running a marathon race to who-knows-where⌉ In his *In One Day—The Things Americans Do in One Day,* Tom Parker details the whirlwind activism of contemporary people, who are almost overwhelmed by an avalanche of unfulfilling tasks. Each day Americans eat 815 billion calories of food—200 billion more than they need; spend $700 million for entertainment and recreation; drink 1.2 million gallons of hard liquor with a bar tab of $64 million, 1.5 million gallons of wine, 15.7 million gallons of beer and ale (or 28 million six-packs); pay $40 million for prostitution; give $165 million to charity; pick up the $2.5 million tab for car washes; and plunk down $40 million for auto repairs. The incredible list continues—every day we buy 190,000 wristwatches, 120,000 radios, 17,000 videocassette recorders, 4 million books, 250,000 neckties, 325 pounds of cocaine. We have 500 coronary bypass operations, and spend $125,000 on merchandise and tours associated with the memory of Elvis Presley.[7] No wonder millions live at the edge of the breaking point.

Though reading the list makes us tired, consider the energy needed to coordinate the schedules and the hungry budgets required to accomplish these things. And what about the tidal wave of worthless results? Our consumer society is infected with affluenza, "an array of psy-

chological maladies, such as isolation, suspicion, boredom, guilt and lack of motivation, engendered by
wealth."[8] And for spiritually empty people, this ceaseless
activity significantly complicates life because it turns
each day into a weary rerun of hundreds of unsatisfying
yesterdays. Perpetual motion does not drive the dread
away or fill the empty soul.

An incredibly powerful antidote for this inner emptiness shines through this prayer monologue with God:
"Lead me, even though it be against my will, into Thy
way. . . . Through doubt, through faith, through bliss,
through stark dismay, through sunshine, wind or snow,
or fog, or shower. Draw me to Thee who is my only way."[9]

To avoid a half-lived empty life, divine enablement
must be allowed to replace our breathlessness and quiet
the soul's confusion. A genuinely fulfilled life is impossible without God.

Shallow Religion Intensifies Our Hunger for the Holy

Many believe organized religion has lost its soul.
Though some are vaguely aware that a moral crisis surrounds them, they completely misunderstand the message of Christianity because they have heard only shrill
marginal voices rather than the real thing. Many on the
street have no clue about the benefits of solid faith because
they have only been exposed to a narrow slice of the real
thing. Some have met Christians who are frightful boors.
Religious show biz turns others off. Others are turned
away because the church is often focused on minutia.

Regrettably, these spiritually illiterate people are faith
lazy, so they seldom seek out answers for themselves at
church, in private conversations, in the Bible, or in other
books. Consequently, ideas about spirituality, piety, and

intercession elicit ignorant or negative reactions from them. Fenelon, the devotional giant of another generation, says of them, "They only know what religion extracts, without knowing what it offers."[10]

And into this equation another foreboding issue also must be introduced. An alarmingly high percentage of contemporary religious leaders have nothing to offer serious God-seekers because they keep themselves busy chasing counterfeit relevance, professional status, or personal gain. It is regrettable that too many lay and clergy church leaders display a sad spectacle of self-serving priorities planned to advance their own authority, control, or bank accounts.

Sadly, these impoverished religious functionaries have created a self-imposed fantasy culture in the churches that one writer calls a "reservation of the spirit—a safety zone set aside for religious dialogue that does not affect thought, conduct, or culture." Of course, the fuzzy thinking and high-sounding verbiage that follows means precisely nothing. These religious leaders, by forsaking their inner moral moorings, have trivialized faith and given up on their own inner quest so that they have no life-transforming resources to offer secularists. Yet thousands mistakenly think these leaders represent genuine spirituality.

The need for authentic spirituality deepens even more when one considers the fossilization of many churches. One insightful pastor reported, "Many congregations of professing Christians today are saturated with a kind of dead goodness, an ethical respectability rooted in the flesh rather than in the illuminating and enlivening control of the Holy Spirit."[11] This summary underscores an anemic reality. Those churches weakened to flesh and bones only have puny pabulum to offer the most morally confused generation in human history.

But there may be reason for hope on the horizon of our culture. All this confusion in society and in some churches may awaken latent spirituality. The need for faith gets convincingly obvious when life caves in and one is forced to deal with life's grim realities. Even practicing atheists often have serious second thoughts about faithless living when cancer invades their bodies, when sexual disease kills their children, when greed destroys their jobs, or when friends join cults looking for a reason for living.

Think about it. Was ambiguity about what really matters ever more glaring than it is now? Was empty meaninglessness ever more real? So much has changed in our values and morality so fast that it is difficult to comprehend the long-term fallout. But perhaps the world may be ready for a spiritual awakening, not out of intentional choice, but because other possibilities have been exhausted. The songwriter is right: "Nothing satisfies like Jesus."

Look at the results of the shallow faith of our time. New hunger for freedom has sent shouting protesters into the streets in trouble spots around the world. Pornography and television violence has fueled protests against unresponsive politicians and TV stations. Teenage pregnancies, divorces, abortions, and drive-by shootings rip apart the fabric of family life. Scientific discoveries and medical delivery systems scramble long-accepted assumptions and values about birth and death. Even though a secular mind-set has a stranglehold on the media and public debate, people still feel alarmed and helpless when life turns threatening. The biblical writer records Christ's incredibly accurate description of our times: "Men will faint from terror, apprehensive of what is coming on the world" (Luke 21:26).

Has the day finally arrived to let some fresh air into our living and to give thoughtful attention to Albert Day's idea? "The power of a life where Christ is exalted would arrest and subdue those who are bored to tears by our thin version of Christianity and wholly uninterested in mere churchmanship."[12]

Maybe there is a reason to hope. Our recent epidemic of powerless religion mixed with moral restlessness in society and brokenness in the family could drive desperate people to God.

An Unsatisfied Self Intensifies Our Hunger for the Holy

Think of the many dead-end searches for a safe place to stand and for a remedy for our inner sickness of the soul. Song publisher John T. Benson described this plight as an "unsatisfied, mysterious me—an uncommitted, unfulfilled self at the core of human experience." Though many abstractions and aggravations may blur the issues, this unsatisfied self shows in our ceaseless quest for our identity. This vague vacancy of the spirit frustrates us. This overactive mind, overstressed body, and undernourished soul testify that much more than biological, psychological, or emotional issues are at work in us. Filling this inward void requires more than we can think with our brains or feel with our senses. It requires an intentional move toward God.

Unfortunately, many seek to satisfy this mysterious emptiness in self-defeating, even ridiculous ways. Nearly everyone can think of laughable examples: A seventy-five-year-old man, after striking up a partnership with an unsuccessful geologist, goes off in search of oil where it has never been found before. Or a divorcée, tormented with scalding memories of four failed marriages, actively seeks another husband while feeling like a tramp in moral exile. A middle-aged executive, though he has amassed a garage filled with gadgets and a safe-deposit box filled with securities, tells his psychiatrist, "I feel unfilled." This mysterious self, if left unattended, leads to a wasted life and a shriveled soul.

But there is a remedy. This unsatisfied self, when directed toward God, encourages the first steps toward faith, potential, and creativity. Lasting fulfillment starts with God. If directed, this hunger for the holy can take the unsatisfied, mysterious self to God's abundant resources for growing a satisfying life. Spiritual development leads to more meaning than one can imagine. It answers Paul's prayer in us, "that the eyes of your heart may be enlightened in order that you may know the hope to which he has called you" (Eph. 1:18).

Stress—Does Life Make Sense without God?

Many perceptive people believe too much was given up and lost when biblical teachings were kicked out of contemporary life. The observation of one of my eighty-five-year-old soul mates squarely unpacks the issues: "I like up-to-date ways and up-to-date inventions, but I still need old-fashioned faith." Though spirituality may seem dreadfully old-fashioned to sophisticated cynics, it is timeless when it takes us back to the ancient, but radical and life-transforming teachings of Moses, Jesus, and Paul. Though spirituality is about the only cure to deliver us from a purposeless life, it is more than enough.

However, several important questions persist in some seekers' minds: Is spirituality real? Is it a mere introspective binge? How can spirituality be attained? Though these questions deserve thoughtful answers, a prior question must be answered first: Does life make sense without faith?

A little Jamaican grandmother gave me my answer several years ago. When I encouraged her at her home near Montego Bay to tell me how long she had followed the

Savior, she answered, "Since I got sense." She is right. Can anyone deny the fact that life without God is an absurd joke?

But let's go back to the previous questions. All around us, impressive clues help us see that the inner life is every bit as real as the physical world. God keeps showing up everywhere in human experience. And though unseen realities sometimes seem nebulous, our hunger for the holy is much too real to be dismissed as mere myth or as an overactive imagination. That is why doubters have problems explaining hope at a newly dug grave, denying intimacy with God at worship, or doubting the satisfaction others receive from giving a cup of cold water in the name of Jesus.

Alternatives must also be considered—do they make sense? Amassing money and possessions has disappointed many people who desperately long for something which new cars, bigger houses, larger paychecks, or fair-weather friends can't provide. Millions, though they may not express it candidly, are apparently bone-weary of religious activity without purpose, brilliance without faith, money without values, sophistication without substance, and possessions without satisfaction. However, for those who seek an authentic way of life, religion that offers nothing more than nostalgic childhood warm fuzzies to soften the harsh edges of pressing pain will not do. People want genuine spiritual reality. They want to know God in substantial, fulfilling ways. They are hungry for the holy.

Spirituality—An Underutilized Soul Health Resource

Though spiritual development may sometimes be considered to be superfluous or melancholic, authenticity and meaning and fulfillment are its main issues. Faith formation provides us with a Christ-focused perspective on life that helps us face every challenge, question every difficulty, evaluate every achievement, and see God at work in the details.

As we open every part of life to God, spirituality provides a unifying center for our thoughts, feelings, and values. It enables us to find the meaning we lost in living, the wisdom we lost in knowledge, and the truth we lost in information.[13] Spirituality, this underutilized remedy for bringing meaning, satisfaction, and purpose to life, when used to its full potential strengthens us and gives us wholeness no matter how difficult our life might seem to be.

Restoring, miraculous cures for purposeless living and spiritual shallowness come singing to us across thirteen centuries in St. Patrick's hymn:

> I arise today through . . .
> God's strength to pilot me:
> God's might to uphold me,
> God's wisdom to guide me,
> God's eye to look after me,
> God's ear to hear me,
> God's word to speak for me,
> God's hand to guard me.

When spiritual development resources are put to full use, spirituality cures self-defeating cynicism, heals inner civil wars, remedies enslaving doubts, and provides recuperation from our exhausting pursuits of lesser gods.

This Christ-centered life satisfies our hunger for the holy. Then all is well, and the Psalmist's testimony becomes our own experience: "I shall lack nothing. . . . he restores my soul" (Ps. 23:1, 3). For a fulfilled life, put that promise from the Psalmist next to Jesus' reassuring words: "Blessed are those who hunger and thirst for righteousness, for they will be filled" (Matt. 5:6). Think of those extravagant realities—shall lack nothing, possess a restored soul, and enjoy a satisfied hunger for righteousness.

Rediscovering and Renewing Spirituality

[Spirituality means intimacy with God.] Spirituality takes us on the most magnificent human pilgrimage imaginable—a Christ-saturated way of living. [With the Presence, common life experiences are transformed into moments of grace, ordinary events become adventures of possibility and power, and life's struggles become sanctuaries and sacraments of strength.] Spirituality is an inward relationship with God that fills every part of living with Christ. Much more than mere empty theory or high-sounding religious trivia, it makes us see and experience life differently. Spirituality is God's molding process to remake us into what He wants us to be and the persons we want to be. When we understand the workings of God in our spiritual development we begin to see the possibilities of an exciting, [rewarding wholeness of the inner person.]

Spirituality—this splendid, wonderful, holy-sounding word—is regrettably becoming an overworked, redefined term in psychology, social action, marriage, child rearing, business, sexuality, legalistic Christianity, Eastern religions, and many other fields. Though we rejoice in a trend that may take God into so many segments of thought and study, having the word *spirituality* too broadly defined or out of focus weakens its impact and dilutes our quest for God. [I use the word *spirituality* as a person's inward journey into intimacy with God resulting in joyous service for God in the world. C. S. Lewis summarizes the ways I like to think of the word: "Aim at heaven and you will get earth thrown in. Aim at earth and you will get neither."

As we have observed it is clearly time for a spiritual revolution in every heart, home, and community. In God's way, a church, a nation, the world are changed one by one. So the words of a familiar spiritual is the place to start our prayer for ourselves and for our world: "It's me, it's me, it's me, O Lord, standing in the need of prayer."

Think how spiritual growth strengthens the soul of a seeker after God.

Spirituality makes a God-seeker a spiritual change agent. We all know our world is in serious spiritual decline. What else could we expect when secularism, materialism, and moral decline are taken to their logical conclusions? What else could be anticipated when so many churches have become inane, worldly, and missionless?

Think how confused outsiders must be by the church. When some of her leaders only a little while ago talked openly about the death of God, the inevitable question follows: "Why go to church if God is dead?" It also confuses outsiders when large sections of the church deplete their energies on controversies like ordination of women and ministry to homosexuals. Meanwhile, nearly three new generations have spiritually starved to death from not hearing the gospel and from not being taught to practice the disciplines of prayer, Bible study, and fellowship.

At the same time, conservative Christianity is not faultless. Many evangelicals have made faith a series of rational propositions, so that the verve of the Christian witness has been reduced to a series of postulates. Though the faith is never irrational, it must be more than a series of rational propositions. At the same time, other parts of the church have choked themselves on legalism, while still other parts keep themselves in a constant state of emotional frenzy. The world needs the church to do more than overdose on liberalism, rationalism, legalism, or emotionalism.

The corrective we need is for serious Christians to fall passionately in love with Christ again and to open their lives in complete obedience to Him. Then we need to ask the Lord of life what changes He wants us to make in ourselves and in our churches. Then superfluous elements will be questioned and many peripheral issues eliminated by our new love relationship to Christ. To be genuinely in love is to want to please the Beloved, and He wants His followers to win the world and renew the church.

Spirituality focuses every aspect of life on Christ. Much of contemporary spirituality appears to be out-of-focus, watered down, and out-of-balance. Authentic personal spirituality, however, makes a believer a better Christian and a more committed, serious church member because he or she is seeking continually to be more like Christ. When we seek Him with our whole hearts, He enters the darkened, secret places. He helps us realize we have almost everything we need except intimacy with Christ. Spirituality welcomes Christ into the nooks and corners of our living.

Spirituality increases receptivity. Though all of us are grace receivers, spirituality is often approached as if it were a sanctimonious pull-yourself-up-by-your-bootstraps. In reality, spirituality gives a new receptivity for us to cherish God's totally unearned love and sustenance, which flows into our lives nonstop. God's spendthrift generosity is ours to accept and embrace.

Spirituality encourages us to receive grace with gratitude. It enables us to see God at work in every strange, wonderful, puzzling, extraordinary, or common circumstance. Then, even when we do not understand what God is doing in us, grace makes us believe our loving Father never wastes a relationship or situation in developing our interior life. Such wholehearted receptivity means we are living out Paul's wise counsel, "Always giving thanks to God the Father *for everything,* in the name of our Lord Jesus Christ" (Eph. 5:20).

Spirituality cultivates expectancy. Remember how much you loved surprises when you were a child? My five-year-old grandson often greets me with the question, "Did you bring me a surprise?" How I love his question! I love his question because I love to surprise him. I love it because my grandson loves to be surprised. And I love it because his question means I have pleased him with surprises in the past. Spirituality is like that, through and through.

Spirituality, the real kind, can never be boring when we look forward to God's surprises. Try counting His generous gifts to you in the past seven days, the past seven hours, or the past seven minutes. Then, as you develop your awareness of all He does for you, you begin waking up each morning wondering what good gift God has for you that day. Every day is transformed into a beautiful adventure with God. Like a weathered saint once reminded me, there are many happy surprises along this holy way.

Spirituality encourages a healthy dependence on Scripture. Too many truth-seekers have no benchmark or ultimate reference point for living. In that condition their own garbled thoughts or some admired guru's teachings lead them astray. God has given us the Bible as a guide to keep us on track in our search for Himself.

I love Marilyn Gustin's down-home advice about enriching life with Scripture: "Begin with prayer asking for blessing on your reading, for insight for your thinking and understanding for your heart. Read slowly, attentively. If a phrase or a word attracts you, stay with it tenderly for a while. You may wish to set a certain amount of time to read each day, but it's better not to set a certain amount of text. There is no need to hurry. You are simply taking a few steps along your interior journey with God. Therefore, read with careful attention to what Scripture is saying to your present spiritual development."[14]

Over a period of time, faithful reading of Scripture makes the Bible part of your interior vocabulary and your thought processes. Such a relationship helps us think God's thoughts after Him and live them out in the details of our journey. Then, in surprising ways, scriptural teaching comes to mind when it is least expected and when it is most needed. Thus, spiritual development takes us to God's Book for specific help for today, but its strength also accumulates across a lifetime. A passage learned as a child comes back like a haunting refrain of an old love song, and that is what it is.

Great souls have written in all ages of the church's history about the Bible's significance in their faith pilgrimage. They testify how they grew in godliness as they allowed Holy Scripture to serve them as their comrade, tutor, strengthener, guide, and motivator.

What variety this guidebook for living provides. The New Testament helps us open ourselves to principles for life in the stories about Jesus, to the teachings of our Lord, to the letters of the apostles, to reports about the early church, and to other "how to live" passages of the New Testament. And we are enriched from the Old Testament by the account of creation and historical records of the people of God, as well as by instructions, commands, poetry, prayers, prophecies, and exhortations.

Scripture, like a road map for the traveler and/or a letter from a loving parent, keeps us accurately on the way and motivates us to keep at the holy task of becoming more like Jesus.

Spirituality provides an "at homeness" with God. All people need a sense of their roots so they know where they belong. My grown son, whose minister parents moved too often during his childhood years, remarked when he saw his great-grandfather's grave for the first time, "Now I know where my roots are."

On the surface, his remark may seem a little humorous, but it was also visceral and human. Built into the human experience is a pressing need to know where we started and where we are going. In some satisfying, mysterious way, the Christian journey provides such a starting place, a pilgrimage, and a destination. But it also provides an "at homeness" along the journey. So we gladly acknowledge that we will one day be at home with God, as the song writer said, "Never more to roam." But we are at the same time at home now with the constant nearness of Jesus, the connectedness with the people of God, and a sense that we are moving toward the final exam and the reunion which follows.

Spirituality helps us dismantle hidden obstacles. Many of us are so used to naming our obstacles that we never fully become who Christ intends for us to be. Our list of human hindrances is impressive and long: poor parenting, siblings that mistreated us, poverty, undesirable neighborhoods, low IQ, or some social handicap we think we can never change. We think we must bear these inner impediments like a bag of garbage that has to be carried for life.

But when we draw close to God, He shows us that our biggest hindrances to developing the divine life in us are obstacles we seldom admit but things He wants us to change. By obstacles I mean unmentioned dishonesties that make us look better than we are. I mean sly envy when others prosper. I mean resentments over slights. I mean gossip that would be better unspoken. I mean advantages we take for ourselves—the better seats at the concert when we buy tickets for four couples, the room with the view at the Christian couple's retreat, cutting ahead of someone at the supermarket, or intentionally planning to duck the check when we go out to lunch with a friend. Of the more obvious hindrances that it is okay to discuss include fear, selfishness, pride, anger, self-pity, unconnected guilt, exaggerations, and double-speak.

Some may argue that these obstacles were eliminated for them when they came to Christ. But were they? If yes, rejoice. If no, please stop denying the reality, and allow God to provide solutions. Try these:

- Resist excuses. Recognize and own the obstacle when God points it out to you.
- Ask God for empowerment, and do what He tells you. The process of making things right helps condition you not to do the wrong again. Like touching a hot stove, the discomfort helps us remember.
- Never give up the spiritual ground you have gained. No need to drive five miles on a spiritual flat tire when you can repair it on the spot.
- Take positive action. Sincerely congratulate the person you envy. Correct an exaggeration or over-statement immediately. Confess and apologize for sins of the spirit.
- Don't let obstacles control you. Own them, talk about them, expose them, refuse to give in to them. The more we admit them and refuse to give in to them, the less power they have over us.
- Replace a negative thought with a positive one. This sounds too simple, but it often works. The idea is to place the focus of thoughts and actions in the direction in which we want to move.
- Offer obstacles to God for cleansing and healing. This requires intentional relinquishment. It is a giant step of spiritual progress when we admit that we do not want to hang on to attitudes, emotions, and fears that harm our spiritual development. Give up your enjoyment of pride, self-centeredness, envy, and

doubletalk in order to become what God has in mind for you.

Spirituality energizes new adventure in service. Christian service is predictable, duty driven, and apathetic in too many places. God deserves something better like creativity, imagination, and effectiveness. But if the world is to be reformed and the church renewed, God will do it through human beings like us. As a response to the grace of God, the serious Christian wants to do something significant for God. This does not mean work to earn salvation, but work as a loving response to God's grace. True service is a love gift to God—one He does not need, but one we delight to give.

More highly motivated servants of Christ are needed everywhere. Too many churches are losing their impact and diluting their witness because believers are arthritic or withdrawn. Others have allowed the gigantic needs of the world to mesmerize them into leaving the battlefront. Still others have become atrophied by the pain of change in church and society.

A close connection to Christ, however, opens our eyes and our affections to new adventures and opportunities of service. Brand-new ways of serving Christ are being explored. In many places young people are seeing needs the older generation never realized existed. Mature believers are taking early retirement to give the last quarter of their lives to the service of God. Some pastors are leaving strong pulpits to work in inner-city parishes. Let's embrace an important principle: deepening the spiritual life results in more effective service and provides us increased satisfaction. Much more than a point of light, Christian service is an opportunity to be a partner with God in changing His world.

Spirituality pushes us to get moving in our spiritual development. Too many people suffer from arrested spiritual development—they stop too close to where they started. With apology to David B. Campbell, as published in *Chicken Soup for the Soul*, let's do away with our excuses for waiting to get started in our spiritual development. You've heard all these excuses or maybe used many of them.

Many say, I am waiting for . . .

1. Inspiration
2. Reassurance
3. My turn at church
4. Someone to smooth the way
5. To know Scripture better
6. The rest of the rules
7. Someone at church to change
8. Someone at home to change
9. My minister's blessing
10. The risks to be lower
11. The kids to leave home
12. A better time
13. Age to give me more insight
14. More Bible classes
15. Jimmy Carter to be re-elected
16. My way to be clearer
17. Taxes to come down
18. My emotions to change
19. My spouse to approve
20. My health to improve[15]

God's time is now. Open your heart. Read and digest Scripture. Try the spiritual exercises following most chapters in this book. Include Christ in all the details of your life. Examine all you do in the light of what you know He wants from you. Give God all your excuses, and sing out in full obedience and volume, "Lord Jesus, I long to be perfectly whole, I want Thee forever to reign in my soul."

May your journey with God be glorious. In this walk with God, remember no event is without His design, no happening without His grace, and no relationship without His splendor. Every traveler will find the pilgrimage unique; the important thing is that we travel with the Savior.

The benefits of a renewed hunger for God are highlighted again and again in this anonymous Shaker poem:

> There is an eye that never tires—
> A God who never sleeps;
> He knows the secret of each heart,
> A watch o'er us he keeps;
> Beholds our motives, foul or clean,
> Knows we are mortals frail,
> And yet we are upheld by him,
> His arm doth never fail.

**Christ brought you over
to God's side and
put your lives together,
whole and holy in his presence.
You don't walk away from
a gift like that!**

Colossians 1:22

(TM)

Master of My Soul
and Center of My World

Help me understand how to center my life around You.

I have an inkling of what that means, and I am drawn to it. What little I understand about centering on You challenges me and judges me. I want you to be the organizing center of my life. Just as a hub gives structure to a wheel, that's what I need. That's what I want.

(Complete this prayer for yourself.)

Centering helps me simplify my life. That means dealing with . . .

Centering helps me eliminate clutter. That means facing . . .

Centering helps me allow You to control the details of my life. That means allowing You to take charge of . . .

I pray all this in the strong name of Jesus. Amen.

Cultivate the Center

How to Organize Life around Christ

> Religious faith is not a storm cellar to which men and women can flee for refuge from the storms of life. It is, instead, an inner spiritual strength that enables them to face those storms with hope and serenity. Religious faith has the miraculous power to lift ordinary human beings to greatness in seasons of stress.
>
> —*Sen. Sam J. Ervin, Jr.*

Steeple-high expectations danced in the young minister's head as he moved into his first church. His dreams were soon shattered, however, by a small, disheartened congregation shackled by inadequate facilities, shrinking attendance, and limited funds. His meager salary forced him to work outside the parish as a substitute high school teacher, teaching nearly every subject, including cooking, auto shop, and physical education. Surface spirituality and raging stress, like a dangerous, out-of-control fever, infected him so that he felt stretched beyond his limits and too weak to function.

Then trivial problems compounded his misery. He felt so shackled by his growing anxieties that he secretly longed for a heart attack so that his parishioners might provide the emotional support he so desperately needed. At the same time, he feared a nervous collapse would require costly hospitalization. To resign would create discouragement for his struggling flock and an additional sense of failure for him. Consequently, the young pastor wrestled through months of sleepless nights until he felt utterly spent with nothing more to give. His ambiguities mounted. His exhaustion deepened. He couldn't see even a shadow of a workable solution.

This struggle is intensely familiar to me. I was that pastor. Life lost its savor as I felt pulled in all directions, often incapable of prayer. Hopelessness poisoned my soul during that predicament.

But in the midst of such chaotic powerlessness, I found my link to the Center when a caring friend loaned me *A Testament of Devotion*. In that book, Thomas Kelly explains how life can be simplified around Christ as the Hub of everything else. He describes a compass that God creates in the inner depths of every human being that is magnetically drawn to Jesus just as an external compass is attracted to the North Pole. The centering that results offers a unified way of looking at the world, clarifies an individual's self-understanding, and provides a sense of direction for living. Richard Foster is right: "We are exiles and aliens until we can come into God, the heart's true home."[1]

As Center, Christ completes our incompleteness even as He satisfies our gnawing hunger for significance. Centering on Jesus as a way to make sense of life provides inner orderliness and generates spiritual energy that supplies vitality for all dimensions of life. In this age of bewildering disconnectedness, such a wholehearted attentiveness to God provides "a handle on everything—a focus around which to organize all else."[2] Nothing is too big or too small to keep God from being life's Center. Centering makes the human journey meaningful and fulfilling. Centering makes spiritual development real rather than theoretical, present rather than past, and practical rather than otherworldly.

Centering Normalizes Life

For some, the idea of centering conjures up complicated mental images too mysterious to understand and too heavenly-minded to be useful. Such assumptions are grossly inaccurate and exaggerated, however, because everyone needs such a single focus to organize thought and behavior. Centering normalizes life by allowing Christ into the corners and dark places, so that a holistic perspective shapes our thoughts, monitors our conversations, questions our attitudes, and evaluates our achievements. At the same time, centering avoids the sterile, sublime otherworldliness that confuses the person on the street and has no concrete meaning for the person in the church.

In centering—this Christ-saturated life—competition between the secular and the spiritual becomes irrelevant as Jesus is allowed to be what He really is—Alpha, Omega, and everything in between. Christ, as the attractive Center of life, is like gravity to the universe, a chip to a computer, the North Star to a navigator, radar to a pilot, "A" to a musician, a root to a plant, oxygen to human life, a frame of reference to a philosopher, a chief executive officer to a business, a gearbox to a transmission, a linchpin to an axle, and mission control to an astronaut.

Even as software controls a computer, a Christ-centered
life sorts out the differences between the peripheral and
the essential, the temporary and the ultimate, the passing and the eternal.

Based on the valid biblical teaching that the outside
always reflects what is on the inside, writers on spirituality use graphic terms to describe how this inner Center actually impacts life. C. S. Lewis calls Him "the secret
Master of Ceremonies." Thomas R. Kelly uses several
graphic designations for Christ, like "the Mastering Life
Within," "the Holy Whisper," "Divine Abyss," "Holy Presence," and "Divine Taproot." E. Stanley Jones calls Jesus
"the Near Side of God." Richard J. Foster expands our
understanding of centering with terms like "Fountain-
head," "Reference Point," "Spring," and "Heavenly Monitor." To be "in Christ," the apostle Paul's phrase, is to
choose to be a love slave—the only satisfying tyranny
ever known by human beings. After a lifetime of thinking, writing, preaching, and observing, one devotional
master called Jesus "the Divine All."

While living in a world where many influences turn us
away from Christlikeness, this centered life positively
shapes the way we think, live, and relate to others. This
Near Side of God helps us develop healthy, happy homes.
This Holy Whisper shows us how to start healing broken
relationships. This Source enables us to give up destructive habit patterns of thought and conduct. This Inner
Presence trades nearness for loneliness. This Holy Center deals with our fear of the future by promising to be
actively present in every tomorrow. At the core of our
being, this Mastering Life demands a willingness to yield
control to Christ so He can be President, Managing Director, and Treasurer.

The most obvious benefit of this integrated kind of living is intimacy with Christ, who tunes human experience
to faith. This intimacy guides, motivates, and resources

the details of our life and work. In the process, centering makes us both more human and more alert to God.

Though spirituality never keeps fog from rolling into life, it stabilizes the inner world so that we can more easily tolerate crashing seas and threatening winds. Christ, as the Hub of human activity and the Magnet of our surrender, helps us deal with unanswered mysteries, joyous discoveries, and confusing ambiguities; all are blended into useful purpose by Him. In centering, Christ invades our smiles and tears, our picnics and funerals, our play and work. This life "in Him" takes Christ into corporate board rooms, company cafeterias, factory assembly lines, computer seminars, family kitchens, school classrooms, and believers' bedrooms.

Centering Shifts Focus from Self to Christ

Centering, an intentional shift to Christ-directedness from self-directedness, begins with a determined commitment to give careful attention to the inner issues of being, motives, and intentions, and less concern to good appearances, images, and impressions. Centering makes Jesus the significant point for thought, speech, and action. Centering redirects life by harmonizing everything around Jesus, the Central Calm. Then stress goes down because "all things hold together" in Him (Col. 1:17).

The possibilities are amazingly attractive, simply because all other centers finally fail. Everything but Christ is in a state of flux. Certain things are obvious to us in our contemporary situations, though we may struggle not to see them: a life centered on spouse, children, job, pleasure, privilege, hero, friend, or self ultimately disappoints us. Fortunes can be lost in a moment from one bad decision. Careers can be destroyed in a day due to a boss's whim or deteriorating economic conditions.

Education and skills can be outdated in a year. Family relationships may be fractured overnight with death, divorce, or desertion. Expand the list any way you wish, and it is easy to see that all lesser centers are temporary.

In contrast, a wholehearted focus on Christ supplies an enduring cornerstone for a satisfying life. Then, when sophisticated distractions whirl around us like emotional cement mixers, this purposeful development of the inner life is fed with the Psalmist's affirmation, "I seek you with all my heart" (119:10). Much to our surprise, even the first faltering attempt heals our blindness, unstops our ears, and opens our minds to the real sources of fulfillment.

Centering furnishes a real reason for living so that we "live and move and have our being" in Him (Acts 17:28). Essentially, this intentional part of centering requires us to surrender the controlling interest of everything about us to Christ—all authority must be yielded to Him without reservation. This means we imitate Jesus' pattern of submitting our self-centered will to God. Then, since Christ is forever in charge without a hint of resistance from us, He shapes the totality of life. That saves lots of agony and encourages authentic commitments to those abiding issues that really matter.

Centering Heals Internal Confusion

Conflicting commitments, however small, generate whirlwind tornadoes in the soul. The resulting debris wrecks the quality of our living. Fulton J. Sheen describes a victim of these inner storms: "While keeping very active on the outside, he is passive and inert on the inside, because he rarely enters into his own heart."[3] In such a muddled state of mind, we may ask: Is life more than a long set of problems from the cradle to the grave? What do I do with my unresolved riddles?

These perplexities between the inner and outer worlds sound like Charlie Brown at a disappointing baseball game. When Lucy misses the ball, she apologizes, "Sorry, Manager, but my body doesn't seem to want to do what my brain tells it to do." Charlie replies, "I understand. My body and my brain haven't spoken to each other in years." That is an accurate description of uncentered living; our interior fragmentation feels like a continuous civil war involving body, soul, and brain.

Holy Scripture calls uncentered people double-minded. From sad personal experience, everyone knows about this war of the soul where every interest of the untamed self insists on having its own way. Like a stormy stockholders' meeting with no chairman, the business self, family self, parental self, and childish self make divisive, simultaneous demands. Such inner anarchy makes the victim fight like a combat soldier and cry like a spoiled two-year-old.

These contradictory feelings are so bewildering that one part of the inner world is active and another reflective; one part noble and the other cowardly; one side aggressive and the other lazy. One side withdraws in defeat while the other wants all-out war. Like Jekyll and Hyde, a portion of the inner world rebels against authority, yet another flatters those in high places. This division in the inner world cripples faith, harms futures, and destroys relationships.

This soul fragmentation causes some to spend enormous spiritual or emotional energy on nonessentials—a massive cause of stress. Uncentered living takes a person down useless detours. To be more exact, an uncentered person lives in baffling vagueness that eats into the fabric of his or her soul. Consequently, a bridge to the Center is desperately needed, even though it may seem difficult to find.

Kelly shows the way: "We have hints that there is a way of life vastly richer and deeper than all this hurried existence, a life of unhurried serenity, peace, and power." He continues: "Each one of us can live a life of amazing power, peace, and serenity, of integration and confidence and simplified multiplicity on one condition—that is, *if we really want to.*"[4] Such possibilities sound too good to be true, and too good not to be true. Our cluttered minds question whether peace, serenity, integration, confidence, and simplification are possible. But when the Center is allowed to coordinate all facets of who we are and what we long to become, these results are abundantly possible. For their life to have meaning, everyone needs this Fixed Point.

Centering Exposes Homemade Idols

Since creation, human beings have raised questions about their reason for being. The search continues. Deep down we have been disappointed by counterfeit ideals so often that we are tempted to believe Shakespeare's sad sentence that life is "a tale told by an idiot, full of sound and fury, signifying nothing." But in our more insightful moments, we know there must be a way to satisfy the deep need for meaning and fulfillment that we feel. There is such a Way.

However, it is important to remember that genuine centering takes more than an unquestioned commitment to empty causes or a loyal plodding through meaningless religious exercises that have been tried many times, in many places. The ancients, like us, sought answers from homemade gods. The Greeks and Romans went to ridiculous extremes, believing that a whole family of gods directed their lives. They assigned war, wind, agriculture, and even sex to various deities, and as new needs arose they invented additional gods. Striking similarities exist among Norse, Aztec, and American Indian religions. But in every culture worshipers experience an annoying sense of betrayal when make-believe or home-made gods show themselves to be deaf, powerless, and disinterested.

Modern people have the same letdown when accumulation, style, and security control their lives but provide little meaning. Though no marble shrines memorialize our make-believe deities, we waste enormous amounts of energy and money on questionable values and passing religious fads. Often contemporary people seek fulfillment at all the wrong places by assuming that a different relationship or a new gadget will satisfy their inner longings. But it never happens because our inner hunger is for God Himself.

And deep down in our inner world we really know why. Blinking yellow lights in our soul caution us against the insanity of expanding our accumulation of unneeded belongings and unsatisfying relationships. Centering corrects these confusions by helping us refocus our attention and interests on lasting values, eternal issues, and the growth of our souls.

Centering Encourages Intimacy with Christ

A fragmented life creates muddled uncertainties. This situation is greatly complicated by the moral short-sightedness of our era. Then our baffling feelings sound like my son's comment during high school years, "Dad, do you know how many voices I hear in my head?" From their own past or present, all uncentered persons know this feeling firsthand.

Dag Hammarskjöld, the spiritually minded Swedish diplomat who served as United Nations secretary-gen-

eral from 1953 until his death in a plane crash in Africa
in 1961, explained the beginning and results of his own
centering: "I don't know Who—or What—put the question. I don't know when it was put. I don't even remember answering. But at some moment I did answer 'Yes' to
Someone—or Something—and from that hour I was certain that existence is meaningful and that, therefore, my
life, in self-surrender, had a goal."[5] At his influential pin-
nacle as a world statesman, centering abundantly empowered Hammarskjöld's service to humankind. The
Christ-centered life offers the same abundant enablement
to everyone—including truck drivers, neurosurgeons,
ditch diggers, designers, and us.

Once having experienced a centered life, no one wants
to go back to the old fragmented way. Even a simple meeting with Christ puts Him in our hearts forever. Then, like
the experience of the prodigal son in the Bible, the Father
is always with us, calling us home wherever we go, whatever we do, and whatever we become. Though we can't
always see Him, we can miss hearing him.

This God-closeness shapes us in an ultimate sense, even
when complexities stress us or life's frustrations tempt us
to be suspicious of the strengths offered in spiritual formation. With Philip we pray, "Lord, show us the Father and
that will be enough" (John 14:8, italics added). And He *is*
enough. A fulfilling serenity flourishes in the inner world
of all who live in intimate contact with Jesus Christ.

Thomas R. Kelly offers several questions to help us
find our way into the centered life: "Ask yourself: Am I
down in the flaming center of God? Have I come into the
deeps, where the soul meets with God and knows His
love and power? Have I discovered God as a living Imme-
diacy, a sweet Presence, and a stirring, life-renovating
Power within me?"[6] Though Christ kindles every stirring
toward godliness, He always waits for our invitation as
an important prerequisite for centering. Our Lord never

moves to the center of anyone's inner world without a wholehearted invitation.

It is reassuring, however, to know that Jesus waits patiently even when we are slow or confused. Thomas, the doubting disciple, is an example; at a despairing moment, he did not know what to believe as he tried to deal with the heavy confusion of an unknown future. Jesus listened kindly to Thomas's questions, though our Lord usually displayed little patience with armchair agnostics. Thomas, trying to cope with frightening fragmentation of his inner world, asked, "Lord, we don't know where you are going, so how can we know the way?" In a surprising response, Jesus caused Thomas to doubt his own doubts when He positioned himself as the Center of all human existence: "I am the way and the truth and the life" (John 14:5–6). As a result, Thomas experienced new hope.

The living Christ did not merely point Thomas to a way, but He claimed to be the Way—without Him there is an unbridgeable distance between God and humanity; the Truth—without Him there is incredible ignorance of God; and the Life—without Him there can be no genuinely quality living. The songwriter underlined the significance of this Holy Center for Thomas and for all who follow after him:

> He is the Way, without Him there's no going;
> He is the Truth, without Him there's no knowing;
> He is the Life, now and eternally.

Integrated living, Christ's answer to today's maddening complexity, begins when He is allowed into the details of the human journey. Mother Teresa of Calcutta makes the concept workable: "Christ is the Way to be walked, the Truth to be told, and the Life to be lived."[7] The living Lord unifies every aspect of our being around Himself. That is centered living at its best.

George Herbert's prayer, though it comes from the seventeenth century, takes us to the Center:

> Come, my Way, my Truth, my Life;
> Such a Way as gives us breath:
> Such a Truth as ends all strife:
> Such a Life as killeth death.[8]

Centering offers alternatives to absurdity, security, ambiguity, success, and failure. Companionship with the Way, the Truth, and the Life unravels uncertainties. Centering nourishes the inner life from the Holy Spring in a minute-by-minute refreshment that allows Christ to bring fulfillment into our work, walk, study, or play. Then, when circumstances baffle us, centering allows us to ask God, Why is this happening? Centering helps answer our question, What can I learn from this experience? In the centered life, everything makes more sense because of Him.

Consequently, the extravagant promise of Scripture becomes real to us: "Seek ye first the kingdom of God, and his righteousness; and *all these things shall be added unto you*" (Matt. 6:33 KJV, italics added). Then it is possible to sing the Psalmist's song, "He shall be like a tree planted by the rivers of water, that bringeth forth his fruit in his season; his leaf also shall not wither; and *whatsoever he doeth shall prosper*" (1:3 KJV, italics added). In the centered life, we pray for ourselves as John prayed for Gaius, "I wish above all things that thou mayest prosper and be in health, *even as thy soul prospereth*" (3 John 2 KJV, italics added).

From these passages we see that a centered life crackles with adventure. This integrating resource "sets the dumb to singing and causes cripples to sprint through a host of cynics."[9] To center in Christ is not to stifle or limit life but to enable and empower it.

Helps for Centering

One critic objected to Voltaire's writings by insisting nothing could be as simple as the French satirist made it. Similar roadblocks to spiritual development are created by many writers and teachers who try to make centering complicated. Admittedly, centering is not as easy as it first appears, but neither is it as difficult as some try to make it. The main roadblock to living a centered life is giving up our self-sovereignty.

Centering promises to provide radical new ways of living. Here are several ways to get started.

1. Think small. Many people continuously seek religious highs, thinking they function best when something big is going on. Perhaps this explains extravagant financial support for television preachers. It may be the reason many people experience vicarious excitement when missionaries tell stories about snakes and scorpions. On the contrary, it is frighteningly easy to sleep through a more quiet, spiritual revolution nearer home. Though there are exceptions, bigger is not always better, and louder is not always more true. There is much good to be found in ordinary days, even when they appear to be ho-hum and routine.

So for inner health, seek deliverance from addictions to the spectacular. Cherish the ordinary. Elijah learned from his Mount Carmel victory and later from despair under the juniper tree that God sometimes surprises us by bypassing earthquakes to speak in a still, small voice. Vance Havner, the Southern Baptist evangelist, correctly preached, "Woe unto us if we are so deafened by the whirlwind that we cannot hear the whisper."[10] Spirituality does not need to be sensational to be supernatural.

2. Make a faith statement with your living. Thomas R. Kelly taught that a centered life is a heaven-directed life.[11]

If he is right, as I believe he is, many of us need to redirect our thoughts and actions to God. Though we don't think about it much, our way of life advertises what we believe. Our choices either give credibility to our values or undermine them. What we believe affects our work, worship, and play; and the way we work, worship, and play publicizes our values to the world.

Try thinking of the truly centered life as a nonverbal front-page headline that points people to God. My life is most attractive to others when I am spiritually strong enough to deal with the strains and difficulties that inevitably come to us all.

To center life in Christ means to welcome His prompting to test our attitudes and activities according to scriptural teaching; then religious abstractions become real flesh-and-blood issues. This Center of Control provides an inner yardstick to use in measuring our feelings, emotions, and sensations to see if they are pleasing to Christ.

3. Listen to people and events. Though God can teach us in a thousand ways, we must cultivate a willing receptivity to understand His will and purpose. Unexpected treasures await us as we probe Scripture and quiz the devotional masters with the question, What is God saying to me here?

Everyday happenings can teach us, too. Amazing wisdom often originates from conversations with mature adults. An unknown writer points us to another rich source when he mused, "We get better acquainted with ourselves by listening to little children."

Listening to events and circumstances can include what is close by and simple. Ordinary things like a bee on a flower, an ant on the ground, or a snowflake on a glove can take us to the Center. And sunrises and harvest moons direct our thoughts to the Father's magnificent provisions. Jesus used common sparrows to question despair and everyday lilies to discredit worry (Matt. 6:25–32). Catastrophic happenings, like an auto crash, bankruptcy, a health crisis, or the death of a loved one, can teach too.

[Be ready to receive God's messages from all sources, both ordinary and unusual. Keep your heart open to admire maple trees, smell roses, or hear robins.]

√ **4. Practice the Presence.** Though large numbers of Christians have some vague ideas about Brother Lawrence's idea of "practicing the presence of God," few do it. Frank Laubach recounts his own experience: "This concentration upon God is strenuous, but everything else has ceased to be so. I think more clearly, I forget less frequently. Things which I did with a strain before I now do easily and with less effort."[12]

Practicing the presence immunizes us against many secular preoccupations.

It tunes us to God; consequently, we see reasons for praise in all of life. Start practicing the presence by asking God's approval on letters you write, phone calls you make, conversations you share, books you read, and television programs you watch. The possibilities are endless.

√ **5. Allow God to test your truthfulness.** In many relationships there exists a kind of clever, deceptive speech, somewhat close to fact, which by flattery, pretense, or tone misleads like a lie. It is possible to become so skilled at doublespeak that others think we mean one thing when we actually mean something quite different. In this age of hype, exaggeration, technical jargon, and image building, it is frighteningly easy to subtly abuse truth. All communication in the centered life must be screened for God's approval to avoid a hypocritical piety and to be sure it is really true.

There is another kind of mesmerizing speech, one-thousandth of a centimeter from a lie, which uses high-sounding vocabulary to impress the gullible and uninformed. Its seductive goal is to make the speaker appear impressive, pious, and even brilliant.

But when we allow Christ to check our speech and our silence, we will be more like what we want people to think we are. Ask yourself questions to evaluate your truth-fulness: Do I use words or phrases with double-meanings? Do I say exactly what I mean? Do I pretend to know when I don't? Do I use high-sounding words to conceal my igno-rance? Do I put family, friends, or business associates off with a wait-and-see reply that I never intend to act upon? Do I overstate the truth because I want to appear to have a positive mental attitude or create a favorable impres-sion of myself or my work? Do I use "I forgot" as a socially acceptable lie to keep from fulfilling a commitment or dealing with some uncomfortable accountability?

Judge the color, intent, and details of your speech to see if it merits Christ's approval. The goal is to please Him rather than to impress others or fool ourselves. Then there will be no need to fear Albert E. Day's warning, "At the end of a single day, the proud, arrogant thing that set out in the morning with banners flying will come home like a bedraggled army beaten and disgraced."[13]

6. Be satisfied with enough. Nearly everyone spends too much energy on our society's entrenched notions concerning money, security, and ownership. No one is completely free from money stress—either we do not have enough, we want more, or we work hard to keep what we have. To deepen our relationships with the Cen-ter, we must view secularism's pull through Thomas R. Kelly's perspective: "God plucks the world out of our hearts, loosening the chains of attachment. And He hurls the world into our hearts, where we and He together carry it in infinitely tender love."[14] That's God's answer to the spirit of the world—commitment to generosity to the cause of Christ.

Since the Father has assured us that the smallest crea-tures are cared for by God, we can safely relinquish our security hang-ups to Him. Enough is enough, and greed is a seductive liar. God is faithful, extravagant, and gracious.

7. Open your dark side to Christ. Apply Francis de Sales' advice to your dark side: "Come now, my soul, we can do better."[15] Too often we refuse to admit our dark side, even to ourselves. These days, building a reputation has such high priority that it never occurs to some strugglers to face themselves. God, however, is never surprised by our destructive side nor by our desire to hide it, because He knows us so well.

Though we sometimes have difficulty recognizing this problem in ourselves, clues increase as we focus every phase of our living around Him. Embarrassing illustrations show up in our disloyalty to people we love, our quiet frustration over unanswered prayer, our anger at God for unexplainable events, our temptation to greed, or our selfish dominance over people at work or home. Author Glenn Clark offers a solution: "Supposing there is some old root—greed, lust, jealousy or hate—that seems so ingrained in your very bones, in your very nervous system, in your very blood, that there is no way of getting out. Then, lean back, and let Christ work the miracle."[16]

8. Resist distractions. It is difficult to hear God when silence has been exorcised from our world, and our households sound like urbanized war zones. Our noisy world vibrates with screaming jets, barking dogs, jangling phones, crying babies, beeping computers, and blaring televisions, radios, VCRs, and compact disc players.

Every serious follower of Jesus in order to hear God more effectively must intentionally cultivate the capacity to listen. One capable Catholic nun, when invited to be a speaker at a great university, responded with a postcard: "Dear, I am trying to be still." A truly centered life requires intentional periods of silence if we want to hear God accurately. We have a need to be still and know that He is God (Ps. 46:10).

One wonderful way to quiet distractions is to think intently about a name or attribute of Jesus. Try Savior, Lord, Emmanuel, or Redeemer. Useful attributes include love, mercy, peace, or hope. Another centering technique is to recall and dwell on the meaning of biblical words like faith, patience, meekness, righteousness, or sanctification.

Many single-minded pilgrims overcome distractions by listening more carefully to Scripture. The following are verses that will lower tension and distractions: "It is more blessed to give than to receive" (Acts 20:35 KJV); "Ye shall know the truth, and the truth shall make you free" (John 8:32 KJV); "You are worth more than many sparrows" (Matt. 10:31 NIV); "For me to live is Christ, and to die is gain" (Phil. 1:21 KJV): "Who shall separate us from the love of Christ?" (Rom. 8:35 KJV); "The effectual fervent prayer of a righteous man availeth much" (James 5:16 KJV).

Silence improves concentration, an important component of centering. Should you experience mental drifting, tell yourself, "I'll think about that later; right now, I'm centering on Christ." Then return to the name, attribute, or Bible promise you were using to help you center on Him.

9. Relive Jesus' life in your world. Nothing cultivates the centered life as much as a continuing remembrance of Jesus. Think often about His goodness, mercy, truth, love, and grace. Try to see your world through His eyes and respond as He would. What would He do in your home or office? What does He think about your primary relationships? What would He say about a trying situation in your experience? How would He spend your paycheck?

This effort to think and act Christianly can be greatly enhanced by following Paul's directive: "Finally, brothers, whatever is true, whatever is noble, whatever is right, whatever is pure, whatever is lovely, whatever is admirable—if anything is excellent or praiseworthy—*think about such things*. Whatever you have learned or received or heard from me, or seen in me—*put it into practice*. And the God of peace will be with you" (Phil. 4:8–9, italics added).

10. Share dreams and spiritual discoveries. Since spirituality needs relationships to grow and flourish, your journey of faith will be strengthened when you share your hopes and dreams with a trusted, spiritually mature friend. Then, too, there is nothing so powerful that you can do for another person as to give him or her opportunity to be involved in your quest for Christlikeness. As a result, the inner flame is fanned in two like-minded people and sustained through the flat times by caring friends.

You accomplish three significant things when you discuss your personal spiritual aspirations with someone: the fact that someone knows your dreams keeps you from sliding into the never-never land of pious fog and good intentions; an informed fellow struggler will likely inquire about your progress and cheer you on; and you generate encouragement to help others in their own spiritual formation. Sharing discoveries, resources, and skills satisfies a personal need and develops a sense of partnership in a friend's development. The relationship energizes both of you and forms a cornerstone for long-term, happy association with a soul friend.

Exercises to Get Your Soul in Shape

- Think small.
- Make a faith statement with your life.
- Listen to people and events.
- Practice the Presence.
- Allow God to test your truthfulness.
- Be satisfied with enough.
- Open your dark side to Christ.
- Resist all distractions.
- Relive Jesus in the world.
- Share dreams and spiritual discoveries.

**Sing hymns instead of
drinking songs!
Sing songs from your heart
to Christ.
Sing praises over everything,
any excuse for a song
to God the Father in the name
of our Master, Jesus Christ.**

Ephesians 5:19–20
(TM)

ℬ

Divine Composer of Heavenly Music and Earthly Harmony

Fill my heart and life with new songs—lyrics, melodies, harmony, and rhythm. I want to sing about You, on tune and with joy. Help me sing at the top of my voice even in this strange land where many have forgotten your songs.

(Complete this prayer for yourself.)

I need your songs of strength and hope to

> *quiet* my heart in turbulent parts of life, such as . . .
> *give* me courage in loving difficult people, like . . .
> *make* me rejoice for those who love me including . . .
> *focus* my thoughts on what I have to sing about, such as . . .

Thanks for putting a new song in my heart. Amen.

Sing Strength into Your Soul

Train Your Ear to Listen for Music from Another World

Music is a fair and glorious gift of God . . .
  Music makes people kinder, gentler, more staid and reasonable . . .
  The devil flees before the sounds of music almost as much as before the Word of God.

—*Martin Luther*

Music strengthens the soul. God invented music for us by inspiring composers to write melodies, harmonies, texts, and rhythms. Then He created sopranos, altos, tenors, and basses to sing the songs of faith for us and with us. His gift of music expanded more when He taught craftsmen to design and construct guitars, tubas, violins, drums, and all other instruments. Like an irrepressible artesian well, the inspiration and vigor of music can't be overused or dried up or silenced for very long.

Amazingly, the music of Christianity can be taken with us anywhere—in our hearts and minds. And a simple act of singing a song or whistling a tune often liberates us from tough circumstances and strengthens our souls.

One evening quite a while ago, Bill and Gloria Gaither's music transformed the Civic Auditorium at Lakeland, Florida, into a place of praise. By singing unforgettable words and catchy melodies, concertgoers and musicians came together around the old, old story of Jesus. That evening Christ-exalting music connected the people with God in ways that cannot be fully described. A crowd intending to be spectators became a congregation of worshipers. That gathering reminded me of a slogan on T-shirts worn by a Japanese traveling youth symphony in the Honolulu airport that read, "We play the notes, but God makes the music."

The Gaithers, a legend in their own time, were assisted by talented vocalists, gifted guitarists, vigorous drummers, and capable keyboard artists skilled at using electronic synthesizers to produce praise music. But something much more than their platform performance, as wonderful as it was, gripped me. I was moved by an unforgettable encounter with God as I shared the evening with friends whom I have known and loved for more than twenty years. The spiritual vitality of the music and joyous association with old friends transformed the concert into a memorable meeting with God for me. That experience provided me with an awesome memory that still sings strength into my soul.

In that short time, the Gaithers' singing made faith real, even as it chased away glum weariness and enriched my parched spirit. "Hold on, my child, joy comes in the morning" drove doubt away. Three wonderful words, "He touched me," brought to mind past miraculous meetings with Christ and assured me of more to come.

An eight-year-old girl sang from the top of her voice and the bottom of her heart, "I am a promise, I am a possibility." Her solo renewed hope for future generations in all of us. Then Larnelle Harris quietly moved on stage and started to sing the Grammy-winning song, "I've just seen Jesus and I'll never be the same again." What a message and what a reality! His song helped us relive Mary's empty tomb experiences and made us aware again that the resurrection stands as the incredibly amazing centerpiece of the Christian faith.

Near the midpoint of the concert, the Gaither Trio sang, "Yesterday's gone and tomorrow may never come; We have this moment today." That song enabled us listeners to cherish the present, be free from our past, and trust our tomorrows to God. The message of the music imprinted our hearts forever and renewed confidence in a future that is always in the hands of God. Memories took us back to earlier milestones on our faith journey.

Think of the power of music in your journey of faith. It grips us in many incredible ways—from breaking bread to making love. Singing stimulates patriotism, motivates worship, and strengthens family ties. Clock radios wake us with peppy tunes and close our days with sleepy-time lyrics. Easy-listening music soothes us in dental offices, on jet airplanes, and in waiting rooms of every description. Recorded melodies over a piped-in music system accompany our first cry in hospital delivery rooms, and church organs peel out our last funeral hymns. Music pursues us all the days of our lives.

Songs so compellingly impact us that no one can cry and sing at the same time. Who can worry or complain while singing a great hymn? And who can carry a grudge while whistling a gospel tune? But everyone can sing and pray at the same time. Feeling gratitude and singing "All

Hail the Power of Jesus' name" go well together. New strength comes during testing times as we hum "How Great Thou Art." Tunes like "My Faith Looks up to Thee" can be played silently in our minds even when circumstances would create cynical pessimism. Often one short phrase from a beloved hymn puts steel in our backbone and in our will. Singing makes faith delightful and infectious.

Music knows no boundaries. It leaps on wings of memory across miles and years to sacred places and long forgotten times of blessing. Familiar tunes remind us of times when a hymn wandered through our yesterdays. Because of the inspiring way music impacts our inner world, hymns are much more than note-by-note arrangements of pitch, frequency, and amplification. The songs of faith help us recall overlooked blessings, heal from heartbreak, and remember cherished meetings with God. The music of spirituality inoculates us against much of the damage that fast-paced living can do.

Marching Songs for the Christian Journey

God wants us to use music to turn our sighing into singing as we travel through uncharted territory and even when we walk through death's valley. The potential verve of a song shines through Paul Goodman's prayer, "Teach me a travel song, Master, to help me march along."[1]

Once God used a song to heal my fragmented inner world as I walked along the Atlantic Ocean a few miles north of Fort Lauderdale. To me the thundering tide sounded like a melancholy melody for my sadness, and my despairing mood made me feel victimized. Fair-weather friends had blatantly violated my sense of fairness and compromised their integrity with exaggerated half-truths about me. My character had been battered by those who preach against such wrongs, but I was help-less to defend myself.

Though the wounds throbbed in my heart as I felt betrayed by so-called brothers, I decided to try singing. The tune was off-key, the words were garbled, and the volume was embarrassingly loud. As I sang with gusto over the sound of the clashing waves, a charming elderly couple out for their morning walk surprised me; and they heard an unwanted earful of my noisy singing. They were kind, but I could tell they found it hard to keep from laughing out loud. And why shouldn't they? My singing obviously polluted their morning. But it impacted me in a way I never want to forget——it freed me from the duplicity of others.

As I asked God lots of tough questions that morning, a line from a childhood hymn started to intrude on my self-pity, reminding me of the eternal faithfulness of God. Inner renewal started the moment I began singing, "Count your many blessings, name them one by one. And it will sur-prise you what the Lord has done." The lyrics revolution-ized my perspective. As I counted God's rich provisions, I knew the song was right. As I seriously considered His blessings, I was actually amazed at how God had worked so faithfully in so many areas of my life. The hymn affirmed my confidence that God ultimately controls everything.

My oceanside victory illustrates how musical praise creates a climate where spirituality starts to flourish and discouragement disappears. Worries vanish when we sing "God Will Take Care of You." Wintry feelings of hope-lessness thaw when we sing with fellow worshipers:

> O God, our Help in ages past,
> Our Hope for years to come,
> Our Shelter from the stormy blast,
> And our eternal Home!
> —*Isaac Watts*

Streaks of dawn shine into our darkest valleys when we sing "He Leadeth Me."

How generous of God to provide such reassuring hymns to comfort us in our most discouraging distresses. Negative moods dissipate when singing starts. Confidence grows when a gospel song squares our own experience with scriptural teachings. Songs of trust crystallize courage and stimulate spiritual adventure as we travel the journey of faith.

Songs of Faith Renew Us

For centuries, disciples have known that singing and spirituality belong together like love and marriage or a horse and carriage. Mental health specialists, however, have only recently rediscovered that music is effective therapy for mentally ill persons. Now the use of music is so common in treatment programs that universities offer a full range of music courses to train psychiatric professionals. Music therapy actually helps people get well. This renewed use of music, however, underscores what believers have known for generations—singing songs of dependence on God soothes tensions, heals damaged emotions, draws us closer to God, and gives us courage to try again.

In times of loss

Resources for inner health and spiritual wholeness flow across the years from Horatio Spafford's hymn written shortly after his four daughters died at sea on the Titanic. You remember the story—they drowned when the Titanic sank on its maiden voyage. While his grief was still fresh, Spafford wrote those incredible words, "Whatever my lot, Thou hast taught me to say, 'It is well, it is well with my soul.'"

His song helped him sing strength into his own soul and provide comfort to his grieving wife; it has reignited hope for thousands from his time until now, and it still keeps us singing in our times of brokenness and despair.

In times of testing

Francis of Assisi, during the dying days of his life, found incredible strength to cope with near blindness and intense pain by writing and then singing,

> All creatures of our God and King,
> Lift up your voice and with us sing . . .
> Ye who long pain and sorrow bear,
> Praise God and on Him cast your care!
> O praise Him, O praise Him!

Now, several centuries later, the blessing continues because no one can sing Francis's hymn without being buoyed by the composer's unfaltering trust in God.

Though Joseph Scriven intended "What a Friend We Have in Jesus" to comfort his distressed mother, the lyrics show he was no stranger to personal heartbreak. His bride-to-be drowned on the night before their wedding, and when he later became engaged a second time, his fiancée died from a dreadful disease before they could marry. To this day, the encouragement Scriven intended especially for his mother revives human beings as they sing his hymn along lonely cowboy trails, in isolated nursing homes, beside hospital beds, in mission chapels, or in cosmopolitan city churches.

During turbulent testings, hymn writers, singers, and weary pilgrims have joined voices in a holy conspiracy against tension, testing, and despair. Such singing either made the difficulties bearable or eliminated the problems altogether. In His gracious provision, God has preserved

their songs for us. Consequently, when bewildering perplexities nag us, it is a good time to sing,

> Jesus! the name that charms our fears,
> That bids our sorrows cease;
> 'Tis music in the sinner's ears;
> 'Tis life, and health, and peace.
> —*Charles Wesley*

While using a song to increase strength in our own
souls, it is easy to understand why Martin Luther thought
believers could sing even when dreadful problems make
it difficult to pray. Discouragement, sometimes defined
as being fed up with things as they are, almost always
fuels pessimism. At those times, it's easy to allow hope-
lessness to nearly swamp us. But self-pity turns to praise
when we sing,

> Strength for today and bright hope for tomorrow—
> Blessings all mine, with ten thousand beside!
> Great is Thy faithfulness! Great is Thy faithfulness!
> Morning by morning new mercies I see;
> All I have needed Thy hand hath provided.
> Great is Thy faithfulness, Lord, unto me!
> —*Thomas O. Chisholm*

In lofty moments of devotion

Ethel Waters, the African-American singer, knew how
to share the vitality of a song. She once shouted, before
a solo at a Billy Graham crusade, "Who needs Social Security when we have heavenly security!" Then she sang
these simple lines with incredible energy:

> I sing because I'm happy,
> I sing because I'm free,
> For His eye is on the sparrow,
> And I know He watches me.
> —*Mrs. C. D. Martin*

Her reassuring song lifted crushing loads from everyone within hearing distance. I sang with her in my mind, and I still do.

God intends for the music of faith to shape us into Christlikeness. Each new trial offers another opportunity to generate devotion and joy with our singing. Henry van Dyke's hymn is so true: "Ever singing, march we onward, victors in the midst of strife."

Sounds of Music Saturate Scripture

In an age when cynicism and skepticism permeate so much of the emotional mood of the human family, it is well to listen to Dean James Earl Massey of Anderson School of Theology, who recommends that we put our ears close to sacred Scripture to hear the Lord's songs again. He observed, "Music gathers up our ideas, feelings, wishes and dreams; it stirs our anticipation and it prods us to place ourselves affirmatively at the very disposal of what the music means."[2] That is what God did when He wove music into the fiber of the Bible so that we can hear His message more accurately.

Old Testament songs

Imagine how invincible the people of Israel felt as they sang, "The Lord is my strength and my song; he has become my salvation" (Exod. 15:2). Sung just after the Israelites had crossed the dry seabed on the day God saved them from the Egyptians, that rousing refrain jogged their pessimistic remembrances and challenged their doubts. Their singing shamed their sulking and forced them to recall God's unfailing faithfulness.

The Psalms, the oldest hymnbook of Judeo-Christian heritage, shows how singing stimulates spirituality. In staccato language, Psalm 28:6–7 supplies reasons for singing our songs of gratitude: "Praise be to the LORD, for he has heard my cry for mercy. The LORD is my strength and my shield . . . My heart leaps for joy and I will give thanks to him in song." The Psalmist broke into spontaneous singing when he inventoried the grace of God. The Old Testament people learned from their long history that music quickens adoration even as it takes the wind out of our worries. The bottom line—God is faithful.

At Isaiah's commissioning, God allowed the prophet to eavesdrop on an angelic anthem, "Holy, holy, holy is the LORD Almighty" (6:3). After that, Isaiah could never be the same, nor did he want to be. The same song goes on challenging all who read Isaiah's prophecies in every new generation.

Songs of Jesus

On the first Christmas, a choir from another world changed human history when it interrupted the routine duties of a small band of unsophisticated sheepherders. At first the shepherds were terrified by the singing birth announcement from heaven. But as they listened more closely, they rejoiced in the life-changing message: "I bring you good news of great joy that will be for all the people. Today in the town of David a Savior has been born to you; he is Christ the Lord" (Luke 2:10–11). Then to add a magnificent finale, the heavenly choir burst into singing, "Glory to God in the highest, and on earth peace to men on whom his favor rests" (v. 14).

That astonishing cradle song for the infant Christ so impacted those first-century ranchers that they deserted their flocks, rushed to the manger, worshiped the child, and went out to share their discoveries with everyone willing to listen. From firsthand experience they learned it is impossible to be the same after hearing angelic songs about the Lord Christ, the baby that started the world singing on the first Christmas in a way that has never stopped. Every Christmas is a time to sing His songs again and to celebrate the salvation He brings to us.

Years later, Jesus hosted the Twelve at an evening meal in a borrowed upstairs dining room. There Christ washed feet, broke bread, predicted His betrayal, and led a closing hymn. Before their meal was over, Jesus sorrowfully announced, "One of you will betray me." With bewildering confusion each one inquired, "Surely not I?" Then the Master explained, "It is one of the Twelve, one who dips bread into the bowl with me" (Mark 14:18–20). Because all had eaten with Him, the idea suddenly dawned on all of them that betrayal stands near the door of every heart. At the end of the evening, the Lord's teaching and hymn were riveted in their minds forever.

Though the text of the Passover hymn is not known to us, it had a profound influence on the disciples. Though the upper room experience must have confused them with separation and closeness, despair and hope, ambiguity and clarity, they could never get away from the memory of singing together. On that night of astounding perplexity, the closing hymn somehow prepared them for Gethsemane, Golgotha, the empty tomb, the Emmaus walk, the ascension, and Pentecost. I think they replayed that hymn in their hearts and minds for the rest of their days. Perhaps they sing it together even now occasionally at a heavenly street meeting.

Paul's jailhouse singing

Clearly, songs sung in our midnight hours always limit what tragedies do to us. At Philippi, Paul and Silas were unjustly imprisoned. The trumped-up charge against them originated from the fact that God answered their prayers for the healing of a demon-possessed slave girl.

Her owners, having lost their profits from the girl's magic, falsely accused Paul and Silas of advocating unlawful customs.

Though they might have complained about being abused and chained in stocks, the Bible records an amazingly different response. After being beaten and jailed without a legal hearing, they began to sing. They transformed their dark dungeon into a place of unforgettable victory, and God was there to accompany their singing with an earthquake. In a short period of time, their heaven-inspired duet freed these unsettling street preachers from jail and saved the Roman jailer from suicide. The results amazed everyone there and continues to encourage Bible readers to this day.

Since then, following the inspiring example of Paul and Silas, each new generation of pilgrims has sung its way to stronger faith in the midst of the toughest circumstances. The evangelist Charles Spurgeon was right, "The Lord is the giver of our songs: He breathes the music into the hearts of the people." Songs of faith always strengthen our inner world.

Other inspiring Scripture songs

Throughout the Bible, God uses music to celebrate His mighty works: a song welcomed creation (Job 38:7); an angel choir celebrated Christ's birth (Luke 2:14); and a jubilant hymn, "Hallelujah! For our Lord God Almighty reigns" (Rev. 19:6), is promised for the end of the world.

Dazzled by miracles and amazed by grace, the early church used singing to show us that it is uplifting to strike up a tune in Jesus' name in both friendly and troubling circumstances. Because God inspires hymn writers, poets, musicians, singers, and publishers with majestic music, neither dreary dungeon nor Calvary's garbage heap can silence the Lord's songs for long. Singing reminds us that God completely surrounds us with His care and providence.

Hymns Teach Spirituality

I love the idea that hymns are the poor people's poetry and the commoner's theology. Years before I knew much about theology or poetry, I sang and loved the songs of the church. They taught me to love the Lord before I knew much doctrine or studied much Scripture.

That may be the reason why many churchgoers can quote more stanzas from hymns than verses from the Bible. As it has been from the earliest days of Christian history, hymns and gospel songs have helped disciples understand their faith and apply it to their lives. The same holds true today.

The old hymns help us remember lessons of faith learned in our yesterdays. To sing "Jesus Loves Me" transports us back to a Sunday school class where a loving teacher taught faith lessons when we were little children. To hum "Yield Not to Temptation" takes us back to a campfire at youth camp when as teenagers we accepted the challenge to live the way Christ wants us to live. When memories and melodies team up, they help make doctrine understandable and applicable to life. Well beyond our awareness, our beliefs are indelibly shaped by the hymns heard and sung.

A significant additional fact must also be considered. Bible doctrine never becomes a holy energy force for effective living until it becomes more than mere mental assent. Music helps make that happen. As a folk singer recently explained in a secular TV interview, a person learns a lot about life in a short time from a song. This idea is doubly true for the music of spirituality because hymns tie tender feelings of devotion to concepts of faith.

It is true—the power of a hymn or gospel song brings faith, facts, and feelings together to teach us about God. Once impacted by a hymn, one may live under its spell forever.

Spiritual Songs Take God into Ordinary Events

Hymns make it possible for people of the holy way to meet God in unexpected, ordinary places. A commuting businessperson turns his car into a sanctuary by singing, "My Jesus, I love Thee; I know Thou art mine." A yuppie jogger transforms a running track into an outdoor worship service by listening to praise choruses on a portable cassette player. A child's bedroom becomes a Christian learning center when a family sings Sunday school songs at bedtime. Coal miners in Appalachian mines meet God as they hum hymns. Cowboys experience a divine nearness as they whistle gospel songs on their way to roundup. And hymns have been known to transform a hospital room into a miraculous healing place.

Shower singing

Though it may not be fully enjoyed by the rest of the household, who can measure what a boisterous shower solo does to the singer? The widow of a stalwart church leader told me she could predict the demands her husband expected for his day by his choice of morning shower songs. At the beginning of a pressing day of hard work he sang,

> Stand up, stand up for Jesus . . .
> "Ye that are men now serve Him,"
> Against unnumbered foes,
> Let courage rise with danger,
> And strength to strength oppose.
> —*George Duffield, Jr.*

He might sing on calmer days,

> Peace, peace, wonderful peace!
> —*Haldor Lillenas*

On a morning when he anticipated that ethical compromises must be faced down with courage, he might sing,

> Consecrate me now to Thy service, Lord,
> By the pow'r of grace divine;
> Let my soul look up with a steadfast hope,
> And my will be lost in Thine.
> —*Fanny J. Crosby*

And at the start of a day when he thought secularism might especially press him, he might sing,

> All for Jesus, all for Jesus!
> All my being's ransomed powers:
> All my thoughts and words and doing,
> All my days and all my hours.
> —*Mary D. James*

An assuring song of faith has power to transform the most difficult day into a victorious conquest.

Singing can unite work with worship

Dorothy Simms' broom marks rhythm for her Christ-centered singing in the late afternoon at San Francisco's Candlestick Park. As a member of the cleanup crew, she rakes peanut shells, Pepsi cups, and hot dog wrappers toward the aisles after athletic events, singing gospel songs a cappella as she sweeps empty bleachers. Though her singing is seldom heard by many people, the wind off San Francisco Bay sometimes carries her musical message across the stadium to reporters remaining in the press box or into the heart of fellow clean-up crew members. The size of her audience doesn't matter much because she is really singing love songs to God.

. While singing songs of hope and affirmation in any setting, the importance of what a song can do to a singer is brought into clear focus by Thomas Merton: "The hymns themselves become the tabernacle of God in which we are protected forever from the rage of the city of business, from the racket of human opinions, from the wild carnival we carry in our hearts which the ancients called Babylon."[3] Spiritual songs shelter spiritual sojourners from the slavery of secularism.

Anywhere and anytime

Before a recent trip, I played a hymn in my mind as I waited in a busy airport ticket line amid the usual Monday morning travel confusion. To lower the frustration caused by slow service and long lines, I replayed a solo I had heard the previous day in church:

> My faith has found a resting place,
> Not in device nor creed;
> I trust the ever-living One,
> His wounds for me shall plead.
> I need no other argument,
>   I need no other plea;
>   It is enough that Jesus died,
>   And that He died for me.
>   —Lidie H. Edmunds

Later that morning, as the jet climbed to 35,000 feet on an incredibly beautiful day for flying, the clouds, mountains, and plains inspired me to think and sing,

> This is my Father's world:
> I rest me in the thought

> Of rocks and trees, of skies and seas—
> His hand the wonders wrought.
> *—Maltbie Babcock*

Then, while other passengers became jittery as we circled in a holding pattern over Chicago's O'Hare Airport, I recalled another song that kept me calm,

> Frail children of dust, and feeble as frail,
> In Thee do we trust, nor find Thee to fail.
> Thy mercies how tender! how firm to the end!
> Our Maker, Defender, Redeemer, and Friend!
> *—Robert Grant*

The songs of faith nourished me that day as they transformed a routine flight to the Windy City into a vibrant meeting with the Father. The hymns of the morning sent me into a wonderfully productive afternoon in Chicago.

Carried in our hearts, hymns, like prayers, make it possible for us to communicate instantly and continuously with God. Cruise ships, well-known for pleasure and gambling, are not usually considered to be an effective setting for worship. But once, a little after midnight, a song led me to an inexpressible meeting with God on the deck of a cruise ship. The full moon, the balmy breezes, the tropical temperature—all contributed to a reassuring testimony of the Creator's incredible extravagance in creation. The wind, moon, and stars seemed to join me in singing,

> To God be the glory—great things He hath done!
> So loved He the world that He gave us His Son.
> *—Fanny J. Crosby*

That night I understood what Augustine meant when he said a singing person prays twice: once with words and again with music.

With memories to recall the texts and stereo systems to play the tunes, we can enjoy profound satisfaction in living out G. B. Steven's paraphrase of Ephesians 5:19, "Edify one another with devout songs of praise to Christ, accompanied by the melody of the heart."[4]

What a privilege to edify one another with songs of praise! Making music in the heart connects and bonds believing pilgrims to each other and to God.

Singing Invigorates Life's Passages

In recent years, psychologists have shown how adults, like children, pass through predictable developmental stages called passages. These transitions, to borrow from author Charles M. Sell's explanation, feel like leaving solid ground to travel from one island to another, so life is "described by prepositions rather than by nouns. Life is always in process: to, from, into, out of, through. Fixed points are few, transitions many."[5] Though confusion is often common in each new passage, songs of faith develop assurance and affirm abiding convictions about God at each stage.

When leaving home

For a young adult, leaving home—an exciting but painful step toward adulthood—engenders uncertainties about friendship, intimacy, vocation, family, and faith. For the first time, a young person may experience the realities of loneliness, fear of failure, or work-related tensions. What a wonderful time to sing "Oh, How He Loves You and Me" or "God Will Take Care of You." Significant possibilities in this stage become even clearer when we sing,

The closer I walk, the sweeter He seems.
Much fairer is He than all of my dreams.
His love lights my way when pathways are dim,
The closer I walk to Him.

—Haldor Lillenas

Marriage and family

A healthy, satisfying marriage fulfills a long list of identity and intimacy needs. The mysterious adventure of building a meaningful relationship with a mate is richly resourced when we sing, "O give us homes built firm upon the Savior, Where Christ is head and Counselor and Guide" (Barbara B. Hart). Songs like this help us grow quality marriages and great souls.

A pregnancy, a significant change point for any couple, adds difficulty or delightful dimensions to a marriage—sometimes both. The developing new life forces the couple to repeat the human drama that has been previously experienced by millions. As the prospective father speeds through traffic to take his wife to the hospital, he keeps thinking, "I'm not ready for this." Meanwhile, the expectant mother grapples with conflicting feelings of joy and fear. At times like this, when stability is needed more than ever, it would be helpful to sing:

Happy the home where Jesus' name
Is sweet to ev'ry ear;
Where children early lisp His fame,
And parents hold Him dear.

—Henry Ware, Jr.

While awaiting the birth of one of our sons, my wife and I endured six months of panic-producing medical reports. Doctors frightened us with test results that said the baby would be retarded if he survived. In the midst

of this cruelly unrelenting anxiety, strength to go on came
from a minister's solo at a clergy conference:

> Sweet is the promise—"I will not forget thee."
> Nothing can molest or turn my soul away;
> E'en though the night be dark within the valley,
> Just beyond is shining one eternal day.
> Trusting the promise, "I will not forget thee,"
> Onward will I go with songs of joy and love.
> —*Charles H. Gabriel*

Soon the dark night of the soul ended with the happy arrival
of a healthy son. And today, more than thirty years later,
the song's promise is as real as this morning's sunrise.

Another difficult transition appears when a couple faces
the simultaneous demands of raising school-age children
and career development. Then Little League, homework,
car pools, school challenges, and vocational responsibilities—to say nothing about financial demands—make life
chaotic. A song to draw us closer to Christ and His values
for this busy period might be:

> In the calm of the noontide, in sorrow's lone hour,
> In times when temptation casts o'er me its power;
> In the tempest of life, on its wide, heaving sea,
> Thou blest "Rock of Age," I'm hiding in Thee.
> —*William O. Cushing*

Middle years and empty nests

In middle years, marked by empty nests, drooping
energies, and tell-tale signs of aging, many lose their way
because unrealized dreams stalk their trail like ravenous
beasts. Some experts think it is like repeating adoles-
cence where individuals start second-guessing issues
that should have been settled forever. This passage point,

where morality, meaning, and money so often collide, affords a good time to sing:

> Search me, O God, and know my heart today;
> Try me, O Savior, know my thoughts, I pray.
> See if there be some wicked way in me;
> Cleanse me from every sin, and set me free.
> —*J. Edwin Orr*

For the golden years

The aging period, sometimes called green winter, demands a lot of adaptive grit. A well-adjusted, elderly friend said it is the most difficult period of life—a time of increasing limitations when one misses being needed and when friends are aging and dying. For many, it is a slow, sure reversal of childhood's development as the aging person regresses in memory, mobility, and self-care. Another senior described this stage as a time when a person starts acting more and more like himself or herself. Loneliness, infirmities, and friends' funerals are frightening components of harvest years. What better time to sing hymns of hope and trust.

With uncanny realism, W. D. McGraw, my friend and father-in-law, planned his own funeral. Because he knew it was his last changing of the seasons, and because the Christian faith was his lodestar, he recorded a solo to be played at his funeral. On the cassette recording, he invited family and friends to join him in singing our inheritance, and what a song we sang as he led us in singing with his recording:

> When peace like a river attendeth my way,
> When sorrows like sea-billows roll;
> Whatever my lot, Thou hast taught me to say,
> "It is well, it is well with my soul."
> —*Horatio G. Spafford*

Getting ready for an exam, especially the final exam when we give an account of our life to God, is serious business for all of us. My special friend Bob Benson changed worlds in his middle fifties after an extraordinary ministry hounded by the frustrations of declining health. As he started toward home plate, he was ushered into heaven by a friend singing at his bedside:

> Blessed assurance, Jesus is mine!
> Oh what a foretaste of glory divine! . . .
> Perfect submission, perfect delight!
> Visions of rapture now burst on my sight;
> Angels descending bring from above
> Echoes of mercy, whispers of love.
> —*Fanny J. Crosby*

What an affirming send-off! And what a welcome home he must have enjoyed at our Father's house.

Hymns and spiritual songs help us triumphantly face every passage with trust and grace. I like to think hymns are lullabies for grown-ups that God uses to comfort and assure us.

How to Sing Strength into Your Soul

Anxiety and fears evaporate when we start singing. The hymns and gospel songs rejuvenate us in some beautiful ways. A few uncomplicated techniques can help us sing faith into the details of our living.

1. Personalize hymns. Put yourself in the text. In every hymn or gospel song you sing or hear, search for your own personal message and application. Be ready to hear God speak through music, because He will. Ask yourself during congregational singing or choir presentations how this song speaks to your situation. Resist some generic application and make it specific. How does the message fit your devotional life, your relationships at work, and your leadership in your family?

Guard against singing something you do not mean, like "I'll go where You want me to go, dear Lord" or "A tent or a cottage, why should I care?" Both songs are wonderful if you really mean what you sing, but they are trite and meaningless if you lack the conviction to back them up. Choose songs that are accurate, honest, and true to your commitments.

As you fill your mind with messages wrapped so attractively in music, you will be amazed how many songs speak to your circumstances. For example, few people can remain unmoved by Charles Wesley's hymn of assurance:

> Thou, O Christ, art all I want;
> More than all in Thee I find;
> Raise the fallen, cheer the faint,
> Heal the sick, and lead the blind.
> Just and holy is Thy name,
> I am all unrighteousness;
> False and full of sin I am,
> Thou art full of truth and grace.

2. Play hymns in your mind during difficult times. You can do it anywhere, especially when you are dealing with trying people or situations that test your Christian principles. In a frustrating committee meeting, I recently focused my attention on the song phrase, "Jesus is all that I need." And He was, so I was calm and charitable—not my normal response in such a hostile, boring setting.

Hum hymns of affirmation in times of suffering, loss, and loneliness. Whistle tunes to bolster courage in times of confusing ambiguity. Allow memory, even in the midst of frustrating circumstances, to transport you to a mo-

ment when a hymn affirmed your confidence in God or
moved you to some worthy action.

Then, when fear and worries are about to overwhelm
you, you can sing lyrics in your inner world such as,

> Jesus never fails . . .
> Heaven and earth may pass away,
> But Jesus never fails.
> —*Arthur A. Luther*[6]

Jesus has never failed and He never will.

3. Sing with gusto. Sing out loud. Shake the rafters. It
is a surprisingly effective way to imprint a song's message on your inner world. Few things focus a day on God
better than a boisterous hymn sung in the shower.
Regardless of musical ability, you can sing while driving
alone in the car. Or you can sing a tune to confront your
blue mood as you walk in the rain. Think of yourself as
mingling your singing with the composer of your favorite
hymn. Sing your affirmations to drive the gloom away,
and it disappears.

4. Try singing your prayers. Like the Bible, hymnals
are filled with prayers of petition, confession, and praise.
As a meaningful devotional practice, trying singing hymn
prayers. A brief review of the hymnal's index will open
many possibilities to you. A short list of hymn prayers
include "Holy Spirit, Thou Art Welcome," "Guide Me, O
Thou Great Jehovah," "Father, I Adore You," "Spirit of
God, Descend Upon My Heart," "Joyful, Joyful, We Adore
You," "My Jesus, I Love Thee," "I Love You Lord," and
"Precious Lord, Take My Hand."

I love to pray and sing,

> O Thou in whose presence my soul takes delight,
> On whom in affliction I call,
> My Comfort by day and my Song in the night,
> My Hope, my Salvation, my All!
> —*Joseph Swain*

5. Sing as you exercise. The current exercise craze allows time for meditative singing, and a song helps dispel boredom during your workout activity. Play a hymn in your mind as you run, whistle while you walk, or hum a hymn as you ride your bike. Housewives and househusbands can sing spiritual strength into their souls as they scrub, vacuum, or dust.

6. Ask others to share the meaning of hymns. A person's pilgrimage of faith can usually be traced around a few special songs that have significantly affected him or her at uniquely high or low points in the spiritual journey. You likely have your own list of favorites, but it is a wonderful spiritual adventure to ask a fellow believer to tell you when he or she first became acquainted with a particular hymn such as "How Great Thou Art" or "Joyful, Joyful, We Adore Thee." In the process, your friends will often ask you the same question. Then useful encouragement flows both ways from friend to friend as you discover the power of a song.

7. Trace a song's influence in your own life. When did you hear "What a Friend We Have in Jesus" for the first time? Its influence starts in childhood for some, but it may have taken on special meaning for others during a time of terrible trouble. Still others first recognized its meaning during a worship experience or perhaps while growing up in a Christian family. It was a fortress of strength to me during my teen years while I was trying to figure out who I was. During college, while sharing friendship with the infirmed, I saw it transport elderly, troubled patients across years to earlier experiences of faith. On an overseas missionary visit, when I did not know the language, I recognized the melody and rejoiced in the hymn's powerful message for all people. Once we even sang it to celebrate a friend's homegoing at an open grave.

8. Use hymns as a spiritual development resource. Hymnbooks are usually organized around concepts like assurance, comfort, grace, and peace. As a resource for growing a great soul, trace these noble thoughts in the various hymns; study their use in the song texts; and check their definitions in a Bible dictionary. Try reviewing and singing all the hymns about faith, about hope, and about service. This exercise is a great way to infuse variety into your own devotional development and encourage you to sing profoundly significant spiritual insights into the nooks and crannies of your soul.

9. Sing dark moods away. During the dark night of the soul, something that sometimes comes to us all, a flicker of the dawn's early light starts to come when we sing,

> Before the hills in order stood,
> Or earth received her frame,
> From everlasting Thou art God,
> To endless years the same.
> —*Isaac Watts*

A secret of spiritual development is embedded in this exercise—it is nearly impossible to fret or worry or cry while singing words like this:

> No matter what may be the test,
> God will take care of you.
> Lean, weary one, upon His breast;
> God will take care of you.
> —*Civilla D. Martin*

The pioneer psychologist of religion, William James, once observed, "We do not sing because we are happy; we are happy because we sing." Clearly the Psalmist knew this reality when he sang, "You [God] will protect me from trouble and surround me with songs of deliverance" (32:7). Make the songs of our faith work for you—sing strength into your soul on your darkest days.

10. Listen carefully for the music's meaning. The slogan of an Atlanta FM radio station—"seek the poetry and inner meaning of the music"—is an important suggestion for spiritual development. Often an unexpected moment of satisfying significance or a flash of inspiration comes as you listen thoughtfully to a song of faith. When you discover a hymn's inner meaning, hold the inspiration in your heart long enough to allow the beauty, goodness, and adventure to satisfy your spirit. The Psalmist calls us to "rejoice in the Lord and be glad, you righteous; sing all you who are upright in heart!" (32:11).

Let's do it as part of cultivating our inner world. Then, when contemporary living pins us to the mat, the music of Zion will liberate us from the clutches of secularism. Learn the delight of singing spiritual strength into your soul.

Exercises to Get Your Soul in Shape

- Personalize hymns.
- Play hymns in your mind during difficult times.
- Sing with gusto.
- Sing your prayers.
- Sing as you exercise.
- Ask others to share the meaning of hymns.
- Trace a song's influence in your own life.
- Use hymns as spiritual development resources.
- Sing dark moods away.
- Listen carefully for the music's meaning.

**Let petitions and praises shape your worries
into prayers, letting God know
your concerns. Before you know it,
a sense of God's wholeness,
everything coming together for good,
will come and settle you down.
It's wonderful what happens when
Christ displaces worry at the center
of your life.**

Philippians 4:6–7

(TM)

Strengthening Lord

Teach me to pray so that I may

    wait when my impulses tempt me to act
      rashly,

    possess steely strength when I am under
      divine orders,

    run and not be weary in my routine duties,

    walk and not faint in times of chaotic need,

    touch in prayer my loved ones and dear
      friends,

    and discover fresh springs of imagination
      for growing a great soul.

Lord, let me become more specific in my
requests.

(Complete this prayer for yourself.)

Enable me to

    affirm those who depend on me,
      including . . .

    accept those who impede my growth,
      including . . .

    quietly turn the other cheek with . . .

I offer this prayer in the name of Christ my
Lord. Amen.

4

Pray Change into Your Life

Ask Christ to Make You Like Him

> Prayer in the sense of petition, asking for things, is a small part of it; confession and penitence are its threshold; adoration, its sanctuary; the presence and vision and enjoyment of God, its bread and wine. In it God shows himself to us.
>
> —*C. S. Lewis*

Tests often terrorize students, and this exam was no exception. In response to the question "Identify and discuss five kinds of prayer," the professor expected members of the class to answer "adoration, confession, petition, thanksgiving, and intercession." Imagine the instructor's surprise when a mischievous student wrote two exams, one for himself with correct answers and a second test paper for a fictitious character named Willy Lump-Lump. Though the significance of Willy's name still mystifies me, his preposterous answers—oral, silent,

93

standing, sitting, and bedtime—sound as vague, humorous, and humdrum as much current thinking about and
practice of prayer.

While God intends prayer to simplify life, moderns frequently intensify their confusion with muddled notions
about divine–human communication. Many misconcep-
tions confuse those who pray or create guilt for those
who don't. The issues are perplexing: Does it matter if I
pray? Is someone listening? What about unanswered
prayer?

Before one prays, must all questions be answered? Of
course not. Unanswered ambiguities surround us on
many levels of life. Though few people understand the
intricacies of medicine, mathematics, or electricity, no
one refuses the benefits. And though few people know
much about aerodynamics, they keep traveling in airplanes.

Is it not enough to attest that prayer works by calling
witnesses into life's courtroom? Ordinary folks and
devout saints from every generation in human history
vouch for the validity of prayer.

Though the dynamics and definitions may not be fully
understood, prayer impacts life on significant, substantial levels. Some of the towering possibilities show in the
answer the college professor expected on that long-ago
exam.

Adoration, as a prayer of awesome wonder, lifts an
individual to an attitude of worship and wonder. It
reminds us of who God is and what He does. Defined as
"reverent appreciation raised to its loftiest terms,"[1] adoration forms the foundation for all other praying. It creates awareness of God's nearness in daily events and
encourages a personal response of praise.

The Psalmist models adoration as he leads us in
singing, "Bless the Lord, O my soul: and all that is within
me, bless his holy name" (103:1, KJV). Adoration and wor-

ship, important components of wholeness, are found in abundant measure at the place of prayer.

Confession frees us from damaging guilt as sin, omission, and stupidity are admitted to a loving Father. It includes the ancient statesman's cry for his nation's sins, "O my God, I am too ashamed and disgraced to lift up my face to you, my God, because our sins are higher than our heads and our guilt has reached to the heavens" (Ezra 9:6). It shines through the robust request Jesus made to His Father in the model prayer, "Forgive us our debts, as we also have forgiven our debtors" (Matt. 6:12). Confession, without self-earned deservings, allows us to be appreciative recipients of God's forgiveness.

Petition, the most prevalent of all prayer forms, expresses urgent desire. Considered by many as the most elementary level of prayer, petition openly seeks divine aid in the midst of human powerlessness and the crushing uncertainties of the unknown. This kind of prayer deals with the whole range of human need, including heartfelt pleas for daily bread, deliverance from temptation, and the coming of the kingdom. Everyone prays at this level at one time or another. Most of us pray at this level most of the time.

Thanksgiving generally changes the person who prays because it draws attention away from self-centered requests and directs it to blessings we have already received. When one expresses gratitude for shelter, one is not likely to be asking God for a bigger house. When one praises God for a loving family, one does not complain about the high grocery bills. When a person rejoices over the memory of a deceased loved one's well-lived life, grief about death's separation is lessened. The grateful pilgrim prays, "O Lord my God, I will give thanks unto thee forever" (Ps. 30:12, KJV). Gratitude cures envy and self-pity.

Intercession, a soul cry to God for another, longs for others to find peace of heart, healing for soul and body, or victory over a debilitating enslavement. This aggressive kind of praying kindles faith for both intercessor and receiver. As an advocate for another, the person who intercedes becomes a victorious, though struggling, warrior in a taxing battle against sin, evil, and darkness. This kind of prayer asks the Father to free everyone from the false promises of technology, sophistication, and prosperity.

Intercession, tough work with revolutionary results beyond our knowing, increases the spiritual stamina of the one who prays even though the prime concern of intercession may be individuals, groups, or even the world. Writer Jane Edwards rightly insists, "Intercessory prayer is not a substitute for action. It is an action for which there is no substitute."[2] The New Testament church strikingly illustrated effective intercession when that small band of believers prayed Peter out of prison (Acts 12:5 ff). And Christian history, from the early church until now, records examples of intercessors whose prayers reformed people, transformed circumstances, and revolutionized nations. Intercession makes a pivotal difference in both our inner and outer worlds.

Each of these prayer patterns alleviates stress, sometimes defined as deadness toward God. This astonishing power that prayer has over tension is explained by Alexis Carrel, a medical researcher: "The results of prayer can be measured in terms of increased physical buoyancy, intellectual vigor, moral stamina, and understanding of the realities underlying physical relationships. How does prayer fortify us with such dynamic power? When we pray, we link ourselves with the inexhaustible power that spins the universe. We ask that a part of His power be apportioned to our needs. Even in asking, our human deficiencies are filled, and we arise strengthened and repaired."[3] Stress begins to disappear as we pray. We find liberating freedom from overattention to patterns and forms of prayer in Augustine's advice, "We come to God by love, and not by navigation." Our yearnings for inner unity, wholeness, and hope compel us to pray. And God answers.

How Does Prayer Change Those Who Pray?

Apparently a "no meaning" malaise hammerlocks much of our contemporary thought and feeling. This growing dissatisfaction—a kind of cynical boredom about money and respectability—means many moderns think something is missing or wrong. Compelling evidence shows up in the evening news, recent novels, morning papers, political rhetoric, and casual conversation at the corner bar among "good ol' boys." But prayer, as an act of faith, dares us to believe that the wrongs can be righted and the missing essentials can be found through the petitions of ordinary folks. One writer's comment makes the issue a little frightening but crystal clear: "Prayer is dangerous business. You could wind up being changed."

Less obvious, but at least as important, multitudes of people believe prayer changes situations and other people, but they never think about how it affects them. However, authentic prayer changes those who pray; a life of prayer involves us in a continuous remolding process by the Master Potter. We do not pray for another without some change coming over us; the change may be in our viewpoint about those for whom we pray, some deeper sympathy, some stronger sense of worth, or some new delight in our own character development.

Prayer unchains an individual from old habits of feeling, thinking, and acting. Having one's inner eyes

opened as a result of prayer may at first feel uncomfortable because "we want to be left alone with our loyalties,
with our good sense, and with the ways we understand."[4]
Nevertheless, genuine prayer—an inner attentiveness to
God's voice—kindles surprising insights, corrects false
assumptions, questions comforting distortions, and
destroys the flattering myths we believe about ourselves.
This clarification also shows us what to look for so that
we see the big picture of God's purpose in the world and
in us.

✓ **Prayer takes us on a voyage of inner discovery.** Like
seeing through a microscope, a person sometimes sees
close-up, minute details during prayer, while on other
occasions prayer is more like looking through binocu-
lars, where distant objects are brought into clearer view.
Conversations with the Father focus the soul's sight so
that we see things as they look to God. Then, in heart-to-
heart dialogue with God, we discover a new life to live, a
new servanthood to serve, and a new destiny to fulfill.
Thus prayer is absolutely necessary for those who wish
to make sense of the worlds within, without, and beyond.

✓ **Prayer shapes us into Christlikeness.** Christlikeness
is the highest human pursuit; it has always been and still
is. The process of becoming like our Lord begins as we
open ourselves to God in trust so that He can restore us
into what He intended when He first created us. Then we
are brought face to face with the essential elements of
wholeness and with ways to develop them. This under-
recognized, almost latent potential of prayer to shape us
into Christlikeness shines through S. D. Gordon's summary of Jesus' communication with the Father: "When
perplexed, Jesus prayed. When hard pressed by work,
He prayed. When hungry for fellowship, He prayed. He
chose His associates and received His messages upon
His knees. If tempted, He prayed. If criticized, He prayed.
If fatigued in body or weary in spirit, He had recourse to

His one unfailing habit of prayer."[5] All these Christ-shaping ingredients of prayer stymie our stress. Consequently, the ultimate outcome of lifelong conversation with God is not what we receive but what we become; the Christ-centered life we seek and find is a genuinely authentic, quality life.

God sometimes sends jolting surprises during prayer—some that affirm and some that discipline. Then, honest communication with the Father forces an egotist to admit absolute dependence on God, so that tensions originating from self-directed achievements vanish. When the proud person prays, he or she is reminded that without God there is no food, sun, or oxygen; that shatters arrogance. When the capable though overly dependent believer prays, the Father sometimes answers, "Get up and go answer your own prayer." Those who intercede for world evangelization sometimes hear an astonishing command, "Give of thy sons to bear the message glorious; / Give of thy wealth to speed them on their way" in the words of a hymn by Mary Ann Thomson. When impulsive folks pray, they often receive a "not yet" answer. And those who come to God with sniffling self-pity sometimes experience deafening silence, indicating how preposterous their complaints sound to God.

Every untarnished, selfless prayer changes the pilgrim for the better. The Christlike possibilities that flow to an authentic life of devotion shaped by prayer are summarized by Muggeridge: "To sacrifice rather than grab, to love rather than lust, to give rather than take, to pursue truth rather than promote lies, and to humble oneself rather than inflate the ego."[6] The act of praying makes the petitioner nobler and humbler, a significant answer to prayer in itself.

Prayer requires wholehearted honesty. Deception and hocus-pocus in the name of religion are common these days. Scripture, however, is brutally frank about honesty and purity: "Surely the arm of the Lord is not too short to save, nor his ear too dull to hear. But your iniquities have separated you from your God; your sins have hidden his face from you, *so that he will not hear*" (Isa. 59:1–2, italics added). This passage clearly reminds us that unworthy thoughts and sinful deeds hinder communication with God. He wants humility and authenticity in us. Every intention is accurately known to the Father; He looks beneath the masks we show each other to evaluate every attitude and action for its precise motivation. So God is not fooled by bad tempers and bluffing sins; they have to go if we desire closeness with Him.

Self-delusion, a cause of unrelenting stress, is often challenged during prayer. New resources at the place of prayer help us break out of self-made prisons of rationalizations and half-truths. In quiet, life-changing ways, communication with God questions our favorite prejudices and cross-examines strange notions that follow us into our quiet times. And in strange, demanding ways, prayer pries into our bitterness and judges resentments we seem reluctant to confess.

Prayer judges integrity. Unworthy motives and questionable actions cause necessary embarrassment during prayer, but high-sounding dishonesty and evasive morality have become so common that they are hardly recognized or questioned. As a result, an educator teaches shoddily during the week but sings in the choir on Sunday. A realtor gouges poor people on Saturday but teaches a Bible class on Tuesday. A published religious author takes time from his writing to divorce the wife of his youth and marry a woman half his age. A television evangelist, after confessing sexual sins, complains on the front pages of the newspapers because he is not allowed to return to a so-called ministry that lined his pockets with the sacrificial contributions of millions of viewers.

This double-dealing even shows up in an auto repair shop when a mechanic gyps a widow on Wednesday after serving as a pious usher in the Sunday services. Additional examples are not hard to find.

This issue of integrity, however, must be scrutinized even closer to home, inasmuch as every public evasion of holy living has a serious counterpart in private life. God, like a military general, uses the quiet place of prayer as a reviewing stand where He examines our conduct and inspects our character. The Father shows us our real self during prayer, the way we look to Him. Because besetting sins wait like ravenous wolves outside the back door of everyone's will, Buttrick rightly insists, "We must live in purity, not offering God an infected arm for service."[7]

Sin poisons the reservoirs of our inner world. The Bible, candidly true to human experience, teaches that moral failures are never completely hidden: "You may be sure that your sin will find you out" (Num. 32:23). While this teaching means others will eventually know about our sins, it also underscores the fact that wrongs keep tracking us down to ruin our self-worth and happiness.

Prayer shatters lurking illusions that fool us into believing what we want is right. Better yet, it breaks down self-deception and pretense as it monitors our temperament and conversations. Such accurate evaluations, when coupled with divine resources for life-changing improvement, revolutionize a person from the inside out. In this process, prayer starts restoring people to what they would have been had they not been blighted by greed, ambition, self-centeredness, and lust.

Prayer provides a long-range perspective of life. Prayer helps us see what lasts and what is truly significant; it makes it possible for us to sort through bewildering ambiguities and trifling irritations. When life seems flat, this new perception teaches us that it is usually too soon to judge whether an event is to be entered as a credit or as a debit in the ledger of life. Think how many persons who once experienced crushing disappointments now enjoy a fulfilling life, and consider how many who started with promise have plateaued or declined.

The grace of this long view impacted Joseph of Old Testament fame when his brothers came begging for food while he served in a high governmental position in Egypt. His daring testimony reassures us even now, though he carried the hurt of their wicked betrayal in his heart for half a lifetime: "You intended to harm me, but God intended it for good" (Gen. 50:20). Before all the facts are in, we cannot accurately judge any situation. Prayer helps us see that an apparent liability is often a disguised blessing.

How confusing that all sounds until we realize that frustrations and questions decrease when our Lord's finale is added to all our prayers, "Not my will, but thine, be done" (Luke 22:42, KJV). This prayer moves us away from a reluctant, guilty acquiescence to a joyously satisfying trust in the purpose and providence of God. Anyone who has walked in the way for any period of time knows that God uses such unswerving relinquishment to shape our future with His holy love and superior wisdom. The result is a better life than anyone could possibly design or construct for himself or herself.

Prayer frees us from self-centeredness. Selfishness, the most destructive issue in spiritual formation, now comes in sophisticated packages labeled individualism, secularism, and narcissism. Everyone, even the most gifted or brilliant, knows how nauseating self-centeredness can be. An overemphasis on self is the essence of sin, regardless of the fancy names or colorful banners we may use. This part of the human situation has not changed since the fall. But after our self-sovereignty creates king-size problems, prayer causes us to assess ourselves accurately and forces us to realize our utter dependence on God. Thereby, we are delivered from sickening self-centeredness as prayer uncovers our selfishness—especially the subtle, entrenched varieties.

Human beings have always sought better self-understanding, a problem intensified by competing contradictory voices in contemporary life. Interestingly, self-understanding increases during prayer when God asks tough, self-revealing questions such as:

Why do you want a job promotion? What will you do with a pay increase? Why do you want more financial security? How will your new authority be used? How will it affect your faith? How will this desired position impact significant people like your family?

Why do you pray for better health? How will you use it? Will your world, church, and family be better? Who will get the credit?

Why do you request that your spiritual life flourish? Will your actions show more integrity? Will anyone gain from your piety? Will you mirror the purposes of God more clearly?

Why do you pray for safety? Is it to avoid pain, humiliation, or discomfort? Will your personal security mean God is better served? Is anyone else helped because you are sheltered from disease or accident?

Prayer motivates action. God makes assignments during prayer with considerably more regularity than any human teacher ever did. Thus, a disciple who intercedes for reconciliation between friends may be given a peace plan to initiate. During a prayer for a hurting neighbor, God may ask the petitioner, "What will you do?" And when an individual prays about his or her marriage, the Father may suggest ways to be a better mate.

Quiet, reflective prayer opens our hearts so that we see ways to help answer our own petitions. Though the idea sounds revolutionary, it could be that God expects specific usefulness from us for every answered prayer.

Prayer without action is shadowboxing or self-deception.[8] This action side of prayer made a Civil War slave observe: "My prayer for freedom was never answered until it got into my heels and made me run away to freedom." The place where we bend our knees is only our port of call, but the open sea of usefulness lies beyond in demanding but satisfying service.

Though we may feel inadequate in God's presence, a conversation with Him often energizes heroic action. Prayer links us with Omnipotence, so that the Helper's strength becomes our own.

This action-linkage component of prayer remedies the frustrating bane of a purposeless life. The columnist Sydney Harris accurately commented, "Few men ever drop dead from overwork, but many quietly curl up and die from undersatisfaction." These days, thousands consider their jobs unimportant in terms of human or spiritual values. And lots of elderly folks believe they are no longer needed by family, society, or church. But when we pray, regardless of our age, experience, or vocation, Christ helps us make a difference in someone's life. Real prayer tears down feelings of uselessness. As one devotional master said, "Prayer is the most important work in the world."

No one can do anything more important than pray for another person. Frank Laubach explains how the hard work of intercession makes a difference in at least two lives: "Prayer is twice blest; it blesses him who gives and him who receives."[9] Then fulfillment and action flow together to enable us to change our world for Christ.

Though prayer is a useful service in itself, it also triggers life-changing action by the person who prays and in the person who is prayed for. The converse is true too; every expression of Christian service without prayer is a terrible danger—a temptation to the ego of the doer and therefore a potential problem for the one who receives the benefit.

√ **Prayer encourages plain talk with God.** Few conversations allow one to candidly express bewildering doubt and stressful frustration. But a person can say anything to God, including expressions of confusion or appropriate rage like our Lord's tough question at the cross, "Why hast thou forsaken me?"

Even though anguish is never evenly distributed throughout the human family, every person has heartaches. To pretend hurts do not exist only increases stress, but liberation begins when we speak frankly with God about our problems. Then our frustration level lowers as God deals with our resentments, self-pity, and vulnerability.

Who has not been wounded by another's gossip or greed? Who has not suffered emotional trauma from someone's deception? Since we all have had our lives complicated by others, God is never shocked, threatened, or scandalized by anything we say to Him. Everyone needs a forum for such plain speaking.

√ **Prayer admits absolute dependence.** People have always prayed in their dark valleys and always will. During emergencies, petitions automatically well up in the inner world. Even in the inner life of proud doubters, prayer seems to wait at some underground gate to be used. This irrepressible inner spring runs so deep that it cannot be dammed up by intellectual sophistication or class barriers. To borrow Fosdick's idea, "The reason we pray is simply that we cannot help praying."[10]

Demanding duties also press us to pray. Lincoln freely admitted during the most emotionally draining days of his presidency, "I have been driven to my knees by the overwhelming conviction that I had no other place to go; my own wisdom and that of those around me seemed insufficient for the day."[11] We, too, experience feelings of inadequacies. Without prayer, who really knows how to deal with marriage, parenting, divorce, reconciliation, forgiveness, or death? No one outgrows the necessity to pray; a homesickness for God always remains in the human heart regardless of attainment, social standing, or education.

As the naturalness of prayer is allowed into daily circumstances, it shows us how to tap into the enablement God provides. This clearly shows in Luther's comparison of the divine–human dialogue with our physical pulse: "You cannot find a Christian man who does not pray; just as you cannot find a living man without a pulse beat that never stands still, but beats and beats on continually of itself, although the man may sleep or do anything else, so being all unconscious of this pulse."[12] Prayer is as necessary to inner wholeness as the circulatory system is to physical health. No one can live very well for very long without praying.

Nearly everyone knows that prayer becomes almost automatic in times of frightening danger and during the demands of crushing responsibilities. But why is prayer not used more in ordinary circumstances? Why limit such an incredible force to sporadic use for extricating us from tight situations? Why not apply prayer to all of life instead of saving it as a last resort? This extraordinary power is also available on routine days. Those who pray in good weather know how to reach the Father during the storms.

Prayer cultivates friendship with God. Dialogical prayer—an oasis of peace in a stress-filled world—opens new ways to know God better. Though communication concepts bombard us in books and magazines, even an elementary awareness of the dialogue process helps us see that conversation deepens relationships. Just as dialogue heightens our understanding of the viewpoint of a friend or mate, prayer helps us grasp God's ways better.

Effective communication, both hearing and speaking, takes conscious effort. But during casual conversation, something wonderfully exhilarating happens when a life-changing idea flashes into our minds. This common experience forms the basis for a psychotherapy concept that says people already possess answers to their own problems deep down in their psyches that can only be discovered in conversation with an accepting listener. If merely verbalizing a problem can open our minds to possible solutions, think of the enormous possibilities that prayer offers.

A similar occurrence sometimes takes place in the classroom. About the time a student finishes asking a question, and before the teacher utters a word, the student sometimes says, "Now I see." A unique factor is at work; the answer came because the student was actively involved in a dialogical process. When such an "aha" moment occurs during prayer, the promise of Scripture is fulfilled: "Before they call I will answer" (Isa. 65:24).

Three centuries ago, Fenelon offered guidance for such encounters: "Tell God all that is in your heart, as one unloads one's heart, its pleasures and pains, to a dear friend. Tell Him your troubles, that He may comfort you; tell Him your joys, that He may sober them; tell Him your longings, that He may purify them; tell Him your dislikes, that He may help you to conquer them; talk to Him of your temptations, that He may shield you from them; show Him the wounds of your heart, that He may heal them." Such candid communication with the Father takes spirituality into all levels of life so that everything, including the mundane and majestic, is magnificently impacted by our conversation with Him.

When true friends meet, every word has meaning. Prayer is like that. Prayer, much more than a traditional religious exercise, is actually an expression of loyalty and affection as friend meets Friend. Brother Lawrence explains how to achieve such closeness: "We should establish ourselves in a sense of God's presence by continually conversing with Him."[13] Frequent contact and serious conversation deepen every association, especially our friendship with God.

Prayer, in its essence, means nothing more or less than a satisfying friendship with God. Closeness makes the difference. Such intimacy with the Father is a thousand times more meaningful than a childish SOS for help from the middle of a frightening problem.

How Does God Answer Prayer?

Some believers have quietly shut their heart's door to friendly communication with God. They have given up on praying because what they thought was prayer has gone dead for them. At least once they experienced what seemed to be divine inaction when answers were most needed.

Then, at the very time when prayer seemed to fail them, they were baffled by the success stories others told. Everyone knows someone whose prayers are always answered: they never miss a plane or lose their luggage; they have money while others are forced into bankruptcy; they sleep in warm beds while others spend cold nights on the streets; and they testify to disease-free, charmed lives.

That may be why some sincerely ask: Is it true that God answers prayer? And if the reply is yes, they ask: Do you mean *all* prayers?

Asbury Seminary President Maxie Dunnam's distinction between ungranted petitions and unanswered prayers helps free us from disappointing emotional baggage on this issue.[14] There is a significant difference between God's giving us what we think we want and His giving us what is best. That is the reason God's loving providence often keeps Him from granting every request, though His dependable character requires that all petitions be answered. Other factors must also be considered, such as our faulty knowledge of God's commitment to an orderly universe, the wisdom of leaving complicated issues in His care, and relief that some requests are not granted. Though God's responses may not be according to our desire, He always gives one of four replies: *yes, no, wait,* and *you must be kidding.*

A *yes* answer, most to our liking and encouraging to our faith, is the easiest to receive and understand. Because few people pray as a kind of casual spiritual walk through the park, their eagerness for answers is serious, often desperate. Thus, a straightforward *yes* from God is welcomed with gratitude. Then as God answers, life gets better and thanks floods our inner world. When such a reply comes, it is a grand time to rejoice and sing, "This is the Lord's doing; it is marvelous in our eyes" (Ps. 118:23 KJV).

The *no* answer takes much more submission and relinquishment than an unqualified *yes.* In the waiting period, Longfellow's logic is hard to refute: "What discord should we bring into the universe if our prayers were all answered. Then we should govern the universe and not God." Though we deny any desire to run the world, God gets lots of unsolicited advice from us. As a loving Father who knows best, He sometimes answers our prayers with a firm *no.*

In mysterious ways, *no* may be the kindest of all possible answers. Think of the little mother's request, "Grant that one of these two sons of mine may sit at your right and the other at your left in your kingdom" (Matt. 20:21). Our Lord's *no* kept her sons from bitter heartbreaks that inevitably followed, as well as the shackles of their own power-crazed ambitions. God sometimes uses a *no* answer to protect us from an unwise request. At other times, a *no* to a specific petition may turn out to be a powerful *yes* to our highest good.

Even Jesus received a *no* to His prayer in the Garden. And Paul was granted grace to endure his bothersome thorn following a *no* answer. These refusals did not harm Jesus or Paul, because they met Someone at the place of prayer who empowered them to go on. The same thing happens to us. This sufficient enablement to deal with a *no* is often a much better answer than an unqualified *yes*.

A *wait* answer is among our most frustrating experiences because it requires passive trust when we want speedy action. In this day of instant gratification, moderns do not wait very well, but because He sees ahead in His loving wisdom God's *wait* may be absolutely necessary. Then again, delays may be required because some attitude or action in us is displeasingly wrong, an idea that scarcely occurs to anyone these days. James offers candid insight: "When you ask, you do not receive, because you ask with wrong motives, that you may spend what you get on your pleasures" (4:3). Perhaps the *wait* may sometimes mean conditions beyond our control are not yet right for a *yes* answer. Delay should not be taken to mean denial.

The issue of persistent prayer must also be considered. Could it be that God does not answer until we are prepared to hold on? Could it be that perseverance makes us more ready for His answers? Perhaps persistence clarifies our motives or helps us identify and overcome hindering difficulties like lesser loves, troublesome preoccupations, or selfish ambitions. Time spent in God's waiting room, often an important factor in our spiritual development, never means final refusal or ultimate rejection.

A fourth category, *you must be kidding*, must be considered. At first this answer shocks us, but it should not be considered to be a belittling insult. It could mean, Do you realize what you are asking? It might mean you are interceding about a settled issue in an orderly universe, such as the fact that gravity always works or thistles never produce roses. Or this answer may stem from requests in which God has already acted, such as Jesus is Lord or sin always destroys.

This answer reminds us of God's never-ending faithfulness and the fact that some things are settled forever. No flippant put-down, this reply means that God is in control and reassures us that the Father has demonstrated His steadfast love throughout many yesterdays. This might be an encouraging answer to fretting folks who have experienced providential care all their days. This might even be the Father's assurance to the pitiful struggler who is afraid his or her requests will be denied. God answers *you must be kidding* to a variety of our misgivings.

Whatever the Father's response to our prayers, He is worthy of our worship because of who He is, not because of what He does. The Answerer always answers—*yes, no, wait,* or *you must be kidding*. His answers alleviate stress just as surely as light dispels darkness.

How to Live a Life of Prayer

Most writers of the literature of spirituality agree that a daily meeting with God at a set time and specific place is highly desirable for inner-life health. We miss much when such a regular appointment is not kept with the Father because these special times provide a splendid opportunity for God to help us make sense of life.

But there is another intensity of prayer, a ceaseless dialogue that puts the soul in continuous contact with God. Someone called it the Christ-saturated life. Far more than squeezing prayer into unused corners of human experience, this special way to live weaves prayer into the entire human drama. This life of unceasing prayer affirms Victor Hugo's wise sentence, "There are moments when, whatever be the attitude of the body, the soul is on its knees." This minute-by-minute, day-by-day relationship puts us in touch with deep-rooted answers to vexing human questions.

Such a prayer-filled life develops a vibrant faith and decreases the abstractions of religion. Scriptures for nourishing the life of prayer promise, "I will be with you always, to the very end of the age" (Matt. 28:20) and "I am the vine; you are the branches" (John 15:5). Such a connected life provides enhanced fulfillment, harmonizes the inner and outer worlds, and even enables us to be more accepting and open to others. This prayer-immersed life makes us quit pretending to be omnipotent and infuses every activity with God's presence.

This perpetual practice of prayer may be described as "in-Christness" or as Christ being formed in us. Calvin Miller uses the delightful term "Christifying," which he defines as "consciously viewing the people and circumstances in our lives with the eyes of Christ."[15] Paul had the same idea when he prayed for the Galatians: "I am again in the pains of childbirth until *Christ is formed in you!*" (4:19, italics added). While this continual devotion does not discount regular withdrawals to be with God, it takes spiritual resources into a dynamic flesh-and-blood encounter with life where we live it.

Exactly as these descriptions explain, this prayer-saturated life makes it possible for the presence of God to bring meaning to the cutting edges of thought and achievement; it affects small details, wide horizons, nagging questions, gigantic dreams, and staggering obstacles. So in stride with God, this kind of fulfilled living laughs at Walpole's notion that our existence is "a comedy to those who think, and a tragedy to those who feel."[16] This "in-Christness" adds a noble quality to every phase of life.

At the same time, this life of prayer exposes the false promises of affluence, security, and conformity. It refutes arrogant pride and questions phony facades. This prayer-permeated kind of living empowers an individual to pursue needed action with courage. Continuous prayer lowers stress because it allows each sojourner to see the meaning of circumstances more clearly and to listen more intently to the messages God sends through so many sources.

This intense level of relationship enables us to pray: "Thank you, Father, for fulfilling my life as I worship with the people of God, as I enjoy a pleasant meal with my family, as I converse with a neighbor, as I walk with an inquisitive child, as I listen to a challenging idea from an old friend, or as I receive love from my mate." Continuous conversation with the Father helps us trade fantasies of future greatness for the disciplines of present spiritual development.

In-Christness frees a pilgrim from living in the drab dreariness of a self-made world and infuses life experience with generosity, forgiveness, and faith. Its resiliency clobbers stress. This "Christifying" miraculously transforms thinking, feeling, and lifestyle, moving Christianity from vague notions to vital faith.

How to Pray Changes into Life

Locked into fixed prayer patterns, many people need new variety and spiritual vigor in their conversations with God. By definition, wholeness requires growth, which always necessitates change. Our task, therefore, is to overcome our natural reluctance to change and to try unfamiliar patterns of prayer so that we can grow into what God calls us to become. The issue: How can creative changes be prayed into my life?

1. Pray yourself happy. While it is true that intercessory prayer is serious work that carries heavy burdens close to its heart, the wonder of God's love generates gladness. Consequently, prayer must be more than a kind of restatement of fretting worries or a mulling over of problems. Our petitions must move beyond gloomy desperation, which deals mostly with calamity or despair. The cornerstone for happy prayer is gratitude for simple blessings like shelter, air, water, health, and family.

A joyous conversation with the Father frees us to soar and sing, even as it breaks the chains of our failures and hurts. The Faithful One, who taught us laughter, stands beyond all our drab notions and weary anxieties. Take delight in God's goodness as you rejoice that prayer is neither black magic nor a blank check, but rather a celebration of a relationship with a Friend—Jesus Christ, our Lord.

2. Keep alert to God's surprises. There are many surprises along this holy way that often occur at amazing times. One writer tells about a little boy who, when urged to write his Christmas letter to Santa, kept procrastinating until his family wondered if he had caught on to their yule pretending. The boy finally revealed his reluctance: "If I write and tell Santa all the things I want, I'll never know what he just wanted to give me."[17] There is a pearl of wisdom in the child's thinking process: God has many intriguing surprises planned for every sojourner.

3. Take prayer into the details of life. Never be content with superficial spirituality. One old spiritual veteran suggested that we pray about our praying. Push yourself to new depths of relationship with the Father as you open every corner of life to Him. Enter His presence with expectancy and respond fully to the assurance of His faithfulness.

One satisfying way to take prayer into the details of life is to form a mental picture of petitions already being answered, so that sick friends are seen as well and troubled marriages are viewed as being emotionally healed. Or, when asked a probing question or meeting a new friend, you may want to cultivate the practice of taking a five-second prayer break; simply pause for a five-second silent prayer, asking for wisdom and grace before you speak.

Another well-tested spiritual exercise begins and ends each day with prayer. By turning your first thoughts to God each morning, you provide a spiritual atmosphere for the day. Or, you may create a sense of closure to your day by offering a bedtime benediction. One helpful approach closes each day with two questions: What was the best thing that happened to me today? What was the worst? How satisfying to end a day by giving God the achievements, by relinquishing frustrating failures or unfinished tasks. Then your mind and spirit will be renewed as you sleep, even as your body is refreshed.

4. Use Bible and hymnbook prayers. Try personalizing the Lord's Prayer. Think deeply about the meaning of that brief masterpiece of devotion. Ponder the Fatherhood of God as you allow the reassuring idea to influence your life. Tell God, "I know You love me more than an earthly parent does." Then ask how you can be a better son or daughter. Think about heaven as you come to the phrase, "Who art in heaven." How does the Bible describe heaven?

Try to meet God meaningfully at each petition of the Lord's Prayer: adore Him for who He is, cherish each new phrase, and apply its message to your current situation. Let strength flow to your inner world as you remember that Christians from every century have prayed this prayer before you, and rejoice that there is a sense in which your voice mingles with those of believers from every century, country, and culture. Who says prayer is a lonely task?

As another example, personalize the high-priestly prayer of Jesus in John 17. Notice how Jesus used the word "gave" in verses 6–19. Savor each phrase of this significant prayer as you try to understand what Jesus meant by these words as He came to the end of His

earthly ministry. What did the prayer mean to His disciples? What does the prayer mean to you?

Paul's prayer for the Ephesians (3:14–21) may also be
used. Note the life-changing concepts in this prayer: "I
pray that out of his glorious riches he may strengthen
you with power through his Spirit in your inner being, so
that Christ may dwell in your hearts through faith."

Another approach is to pray St. Francis's prayer, which
has been set to music:

> Lord, make me an instrument of Thy peace.
> Where there is hatred, let me sow love;
> Where there is injury, pardon;
> Where there is doubt, faith;
> Where there is despair, hope;
> Where there is darkness, light;
> And where there is sadness, joy.

New vistas of spiritual insights open as you spend a half
hour applying Francis's petition to your life.

"Guide Me, O Thou Great Jehovah" by William Williams
is an example of a hymn prayer. The opening line petitions, "Guide me, O Thou great Jehovah, / Pilgrim through
this barren land." As you pray the hymn, ask God to help
you accept divine leadership. How have you received
guidance? How well do you follow His leadership? Next,
think of the implications of the phrase, "O Thou great
Jehovah." Then add, "Pilgrims through this barren land."
Turn next to the reassuring line, so full of worship potential, "I am weak, but Thou art mighty; / Hold me with Thy
powerful hand."

The spiritual nurture possibilities from the prayers of
the Bible and hymnal are nearly limitless. Explore them
often to grow spiritually strong.

5. Cultivate thanks for trifles and troubles. Prayer
helps us sort out the difference between inconveniences

and real problems. Since thousands of small blessings add up to make life wonderful, express gratitude for routine provisions like a tasty meal, a friendly letter, a cheery greeting, a baby's grin, or an autumn picnic. Why not make ordinary circumstances or even petty annoyances reasons for thanks?

Try viewing troubles with gratitude. Consider problems as growth opportunities, and pray with thanksgiving for difficulties. A sprained ankle slows you down for reflection, a misunderstanding allows you the grace of giving and receiving forgiveness, and a financial problem teaches deeper dependence on God. A failed business deal, a wait in the doctor's office, or a traffic snarl can be turned into a channel of grace to draw you closer to Christ, to slow you down, or to increase your patience.

Trials often provide teachable moments and valuable lessons. Richard Foster advises, "The dark night is one of the ways God brings us to a hush, a stillness, so that He may work an inner transformation upon the soul."[18]

6. Listen more intently to God. In our impatience and inexperience with silence, we sometimes make prayer a monologue rather than a dialogue; we fill the time of prayer with a string of high-sounding words rather than letting Scripture resonate within us. The ability to listen in both the inner and outer life requires a willingness to hear and a discipline to listen. As Pamela Gray reminds us, "For one soul that exclaims, 'Speak, Lord, for Thy servant heareth,' there are ten that say, 'Hear, Lord, for Thy servant speaketh.'"

Your life, like most moderns, is probably too noisy. It is difficult to find time or space for reflection when our days start with a ringing alarm, continue with jarring morning news, traffic confusion on the way to work, and loud ruckus on the job, and then end with more snarled traffic. Even though the Psalmist never lived with the intensity of our stress, he recommends, "Be still, and

know that I am God" (46:10). That means thinking, looking beneath the surface, checking our experiences, and
judging our ideas against Scripture. Every disciple of
Christ needs to hear God say more about his or her life.

To be spiritually healthy, we must occasionally withdraw from the daily grind to a block of quiet time where
we drop every hint of resistance and listen to God with
every fiber of our being. Consider Dom Helder Camara's
sobering sentence: "The noise that completely smothers
the voice of God is the inner uproar of outraged self-
esteem, of awakening suspicion, of unsleeping ambition."
Those who quiet themselves find recuperative renewal
awaiting them in the simple fact that some of life's most
confusing riddles can only be solved by intense listening. This exercise makes vital the scriptural directive,
"Wait on the Lord" (Ps. 27:14 KJV). To really know God,
the bedrock foundation of everything else, takes stillness
and time. As Martin Luther explained, "The fewer the
words, the better the prayer."

7. Pray all the time. Dolly of the Family Circus cartoon
speaks with childlike wisdom when she tells her little
brother, "We can talk to God anytime we want because
He has a toll-free number." She is right, and we can have
a special closeness in prayer that takes God into awk-
ward situations when others may be angry, worried, or
even unreasonable. Steve Harper says that John Wesley
tuned his "inner voice" to the Creator.[19] Nearly every situation, however tense, can be turned into an inner conversation with the Father—even when others falsely
accuse us, when people gossip about us, when we are in
the middle of family tensions or workplace stresses. Constant contact with Christ lowers stress; the possibilities
are magnificent.

8. Recognize a need for prayer breaks. Every feeling
of stress or awareness of tension is a signal to pray. Look
carefully for subtle clues that remind you that you need

to pray. Because busyness can shrivel the soul, it is important to recognize the desirability of frequent prayer breaks. Our petty reactions to people provide reminders. Nonverbal messages from others may alert us, and sometimes our bodies inform us that it is time to pray. Another embarrassing hint comes whenever we are forced to make excuses for our conduct. As we keep alert to God and our surroundings, internal messages remind us when a prayer break is needed.

9. Expand your prayer repertoire. One learns to pray by praying. Experiment with several ways of praying; one may fit your needs better at one time than at another. Try adoration, confession, petition, gratitude, and intercession—at least one of these prayer patterns may be unfamiliar to you. Commit yourself to a different kind of prayer each day for a week. You will find spiritual development deepens as your prayer patterns expand. Move from mechanics to meditation, from regimentation to relationship, from methods to mastery. Which kind of prayer do you most need? Which prayer pattern is least familiar to you?

God encourages individuality and authenticity when He offers us this wide range of approaches in our communication with Him. Though monotony, rigidity, and empty forms are deadly enemies of spiritual growth, the disciplines of prayer, worship, and fasting can be vibrant and even liberating. Use variety in prayer to help satisfy your quest to be Christlike.

10. Pray correction into your life. In our most insightful moments, it is refreshingly amazing to realize that we are unfinished products being drawn to completion by God—someone called it stretching for the stars while standing on the earth. Consequently, during prayer God often identifies improvements He wants us to make as He calls us to something more than a sentimental faith and a lukewarm devotion. Every change the Father proposes must be seen for what it really is—for our good. But Bob Benson is right: "When we pray, we have to change. We have to be different that day. We have to treat people differently. We have to act differently. We walk differently." He continues, for some "it's just easier not to pray. It's just easier not to have His eyes and His heart."[20]

God's insistent nudges toward improvement usually come during quiet prayer, while reading Scripture, in the midst of an unusual life experience, during a chance conversation, while listening to a sermon, or while thinking about the text of a hymn. The Westminster Shorter Catechism summarizes the issue: "Prayer is an offering of our desires unto God, for things agreeable to His will." Caught up in the glorious possibilities of spiritual development, during prayer we discover God's enablement for every correction He urges, so our requests can be shaped into things agreeable to His will.

Exercises to Get Your Soul in Shape

- Pray yourself happy.
- Keep alert to God's surprises.
- Take prayer into the details of life.
- Use Bible and hymnbook prayers.
- Cultivate thanks for trifles and troubles.
- Listen more intently to God.
- Pray all the time.
- Recognize a need for prayer breaks.
- Expand your prayer repertoire.
- Pray correction into your life.

**My times
are in
your hands.**

Psalm 31:15

(NIV)

૪૭

Giver and Ruler of All My Days

I thank You for giving me time to
live a spiritually adventuresome life,
make a significant impact on another's pilgrimage,
smell the flowers and climb the summits,
experience grace and give mercy, and
cherish Your greatness and receive Your
  forgiveness.

(Complete this prayer for yourself.)

I need divine enablement to prioritize my life so
I can

accomplish these ministries . . .
invest my life and love and vision in . . .
be more useful to You in these ways . . .
  Thank you for helping me use my time to
cultivate a beautiful life. Amen.

Make Time Your Friend

Do Something Wonderful with Every Day

It is difficult to live in the present, ridiculous to live in the future, and impossible to live in the past. Nothing is as far away as one minute ago.

—*Jim Bishop*

Clocks, schedules, and calendars scramble our thoughts about the good life, so we try to get more done in less and less time. Time often tricks us; on some days it races like a marathon runner, but on other days it loiters along like a lazy bum. Overcrowded schedules make us feel like Jeffy in the Family Circus cartoon: "Whenever I can't wait until tomorrow, it is yesterday."

Many of these ambivalent feelings about time were captured by an Appalachian radio announcer who opened the country radio station one morning with the unnerving remark, "If you are lucky, you get a little older every day." All our topsy-turvy misgivings about time make us anxious about the past and afraid of the future. Many think of time as an uncontrollable monster, while others believe they benefit from fast-passing time because it forces them to weed out trivia.

This predicament of life running too slow or too fast confronts all of us during some stage in our lives. Night passes at a snail's pace for an insomniac, yet next Christmas seems like a hundred years away for the little girl next door. That explains why five years in the future seems like tomorrow to a busy executive. High school graduation sounds like light-years away for a kindergartner, while those twelve years will pass like an eye blink for the child's grandmother. An hour crawls slowly in the dentist's chair, but flies incredibly fast under a romantic moon. For most of us, our problems with time get serious at some mysterious moment near the end of childhood when life seems to shift into high gear. And too soon we come to retirement years wondering why it takes such a short time to live a lifetime.

These frightening time puzzles and our reactions to them are reflected in Michael Quoist's prayer, "Lord, you must have made some error in your calculation. There is a big mistake somewhere. The hours are too short, the days are too short, our lives are too short."[1] Apparently many people think life would be considerably less complicated if they had more time because they feel as if they are falling behind as they strive to get ahead. As we meet ourselves coming and going, time must be seen as an ally to cultivate rather than an adversary to fight.

Time's Baffling Quirks

Time, a raw material of everything else, has many fascinating quirks. Time heals wounds, equalizes many things, and is generally in short supply. Trying to make sense of these beguiling distortions, Frederick Buechner remarked, "So often for many of us—all of us, really—life floats in one eye and out the other. If you asked me what I did yesterday, I'd find it hard to tell you."[2] Like a frantic seamstress, time specializes in alterations.

Though everyone knows time is the basic stuff for building a satisfying life, long years of living do not guarantee a meaningful existence, and life in the fast lane gets us to the end too soon.

All these eccentricities keep us guessing and confused. Every minute has 60 seconds, every day has 24 hours, and every year has 365 days—it is supposed to be the same for everyone. But time allocations are grossly unfair to those who die at twenty compared with those who live past eighty.

On the opposite end of the spectrum, a recent scientific survey of five thousand adults shows Americans have more free time than ever. A contradictory survey shows that leisure time has shrunk by 37 percent since 1973 and that the average workweek has jumped to 47 hours.

All this confusion deepens still more when we consider how a person squanders hours and days but cannot hoard, earn, or borrow one minute. Time can be spent but not bought, saved but not stockpiled, given but never loaned. Time can be remembered but not reversed. You can waste a lifetime but not create an extra hour.

This freakish irony intensifies: Time waits for no one, but nobody knows where it goes. We stew over questions about time such as, Why do we work so hard? Why are we out of breath when we have dryers for our clothes, cars for our travel, and computers to streamline our businesses? What happened to the timesaving promises of fax machines, robotics, and other wizardries? Who or what can we blame for this famine of time?

Our bafflement about time shows in the amazing custom of presenting gold watches to retirees who no longer need to keep track of time. Though it takes only a short time to live a lifetime, the average person wastes enough hours in a decade to earn a college degree.

Acceleration, among the most stress-producing issues in contemporary society, means that moderns sprint for planes, push ahead in supermarket lines, and fume in rush-hour traffic. Our timesaving gadgets fast-forward, dub, split-screen, and record—benefits we did not know we needed twenty years ago. In this dizzying state of affairs, the marketplace is cluttered with time management gimmicks like trendy datebooks, beguiling organizational calendars, expensive high-tech watches, confusing mini-computers, and intensive time management seminars. Yet in spite of all this bustle, time eludes us. We are forced to agree with an unknown writer's conclusion, "Time is like a circus, always packing up and moving away."

Delusions and false hopes fog the facts about time while our so-called shortcut schedules fill every minute to the brim. We are captives to our cellular phones, answering machines, and personal computers as well as to the time required to earn more money to buy things we do not need. All this makes us chuckle when we read the hotel elevator sign, "This is the tomorrow you worried about yesterday." As we consider all these time issues, our own rat race makes us nod in agreement with the anonymous pessimist who penciled at the bottom of the sign, "Now we know why."

Convincing indicators can be seen everywhere that real satisfaction in all of life depends on whether we choose to make time our adversary or friend.

What Is Time For?

Time, the landscape of experience, according to Francis Bacon, might be considered the bricks and lumber for building a life of satisfying achievements and fulfilling relationships. That means stress-causing irritations are constantly felt by those who think they have too much or too little time—that includes nearly everybody.

Surprisingly, the determining cause of our stress about time appears to be within ourselves. Two people have similar jobs—one is relaxed, with enough time for work and play, while the other is always breathlessly busy. Nearly everyone knows that what we do with time is more important than its duration. Time for family, meals, sickness, and marriage is out of control for many people; consequently, the finished product we desire most gets squeezed to the very periphery of our lives because we seldom allocate adequate time for reflection, creativity, or God.

If all of this is accurate, the complications of our busyness can be lessened when we cultivate time as a cherished friend rather than fearing it as a threatening taskmaster. Though such a decision appears easy to make, it is actually revolutionary because it is the first step toward viewing time as a gem to treasure, a joy to give, or even a luxury to squander. However, no combination of gadgets, innovations, or helpful insights will automatically nurture a happy friendship with time.

Perhaps it is time to wake up to what our compulsions about schedules and calendars are doing to us. At some point an individual must consider the toll that busyness takes on the emotions and spirit. It is amazing, but true, that spiritual development must become a high priority in our use of time before we can accurately decide what else is important to us.

As the various alternatives are considered, we are likely to be attracted to the Jesus way, which Pastor Milo Arnold explains in these two sentences: "Jesus didn't need longer days nor extended years. He just took the time He had and fitted life into it so well that His work was done when His time was gone."[3] Clearly, our Lord never postponed a task because of lack of time, but still enjoyed a satisfying life. Consequently, Jesus stands as a worthy model for effective use of time.

The investment of quality time is the price one pays for meaning. To begin developing a friendship with time, one starts by sorting out the difference between hurry and satisfaction, between the urgent and the significant, and between the pressing and the eternal. Gandhi, the Hindu statesman, understood this point and taught that "There is more to life than increasing its speed." Our task, therefore, is to find ways to live better instead of packing more activities into our overstuffed calendars.

Perhaps the most basic ingredient for building a quality life is recognition that each time segment has incredible potential for fulfillment, and schedules cannot control us without our consent. Thus weary, hassled people must reverse their ideas about being prisoners of time. Time does not chase us with a dagger, nor does it hold us as captive slaves. We all have more control of our time than we think. The American humorist Will Rogers was right: "Half our life is spent trying to find something to do with the time we have rushed through life trying to save."

Though it may be hard to believe, the whole world can get along without any one of us for five minutes or longer. It did before we were born, and it will survive after we are gone.

To begin thinking in new ways about your use of time and your feelings about it, why not consider time as a basket filled with possibilities for fulfillment and power for renewal? Commit to the liberating notion that regret about the past will never take you forward. Plainly, then, new days, new weeks, and new seasons will remind us that we live surrounded by fresh beginnings that provide possibilities to help us get better acquainted with God. This is the reason that it is so important to occasionally step off the whirling treadmill to catch our breath, to nurture our soul, and to put our ear close to life so that we are able to hear what God says through a thousand different voices about the way we use time.

Time Enough for What Really Matters

Squandered minutes waste life. Carl Sandburg, two-time Pulitzer prize–winning poet, expresses an uncomfortable but accurate thought about our mind-numbing schedules: "Time is the coin of your life. It is the only coin you have and only you can determine how it will be spent. Be careful lest you let others spend it for you." Though life without intentional priorities evaporates like water on desert sand, few people seem to be able to invest time wisely.

Therefore, we need to make thoughtful decisions about our use of time for at least two reasons: first, it is our personal possession—it belongs only to us; second, it is limited—no one can get more time.

Consequently, the way we prioritize time determines whether we will have few dull moments or many long-term regrets. A quality life takes time; a satisfying life takes more time; and a great, fulfilling life takes even more time. The writer of Ecclesiastes believed everything has an ideal time, and the accuracy of his insight eventually dawns on every serious seeker after God. The idea is amplified in poetic language by dramatist Edmund Rostrand: "There is a time when beauty stands staring into the soul with sad, sweet eyes that sicken at the sounds of words. And God help those who pass that moment by."

Building a happy relationship with time determines whether we stagger through life or journey with a satisfying purpose toward meaning and fulfillment. Indeed, every time segment, however short or long, possesses possibilities for helping us live fully and hopefully. Time is ours; only truly significant issues are worth large investments of our time.

Models for Making Friends with Time

Let me introduce several common, though extraordinary people, who cultivated a happy friendship with time by refusing to squander the bits and pieces of their lives. Though they probably never read George Bernard Shaw's writings, they embraced his idea that "the greatest joy is to be used by a purpose you recognize as a mighty one."

Martin Paulson chose, in his retirement years, to be a substitute grandfather to my preschool sons, who lived hundreds of miles from their natural grandparents. These boys, now grown men, learned how to saw and hammer from Grandpa Paulson. Beyond that, they experienced the delightfully enriching benefit of a spellbinding relationship with an adult friend. Martin intuitively followed Paul's advice, "Let love guide your life" (Col. 3:14, TLB). Who can calculate his impact on the children or measure the fulfillment he enjoyed by giving them the gift of himself?

In their late twenties, Margie and Paul Kemp moved into cramped University of Michigan campus housing with three grade-school-age sons to pursue education degrees that had earlier seemed unimportant. Later, after years of classroom teaching and after earning advanced degrees, Paul was promoted to a high-level educational post where he continues to be an influential key player in formulating public school policy affecting thousands of children. Margie, in her too-short lifetime, worked miracles with speech-handicapped preschool children, so that some of her so-called learning disabled kids have since graduated with honors from college. By investing in children, Margie and Paul learned that immense satisfaction comes from giving time away. In the process they made the world better.

Madge Watson, after a long career as an administrative assistant to a Holly Sugar Corporation executive, thought retirement was a waste of her time. Well beyond sixty-five, she became a Girl Friday for a small church, where she operated a temperamental copy machine, answered phone calls, and replied to questions about the church-operated preschool. On purpose, Madge used her senior years to discover a gratifying life many people never know.

Following the death of his twenty-year-old daughter from leukemia, Wayne Sparling, master metal craftsman, took massive chunks of time away from his thriving business to design, build, and install a steeple for his church as productive grief work. His gift of time became a fitting tribute to Nancy's life because this work of art will draw the community and church closer to God for years into the future. Who can compute the impact of his time gift?

Like Martha of the Bible, Clara Underwood served the senior adults of her church, giving special attention to Elizabeth Cullin during her long, losing battle with cancer. Equally at home in her garden or a sickroom, Clara took a homegrown rose to Mrs. Cullin every day and practiced her conviction that time is a strength to be given to those who need it most.

Mary Quackenbush refused to allow her advancing years to slow her down to a life of respectable ease. After renewing her faith-commitment at age seventy-five, she started out on a twelve-year effort for Christ, becoming a well-loved spiritual mother to a whole congregation. She packed each week full of service by counting the church offerings on Monday, leading a Bible study for

women in her home on Tuesday, calling on lonely hos-
pitalized people all day Wednesday, heading a visitation
team on Thursday evenings, and teaching a Bible class
for preteen girls on Sunday mornings. She added vigor
and joy to her years by serving others.

From firsthand experience, these people found living
out Jesus' teaching to be time-consuming but satisfying:
"Whoever wants to become great among you must be
your servant" (Mark 10:43). They deepened friendships
with time by giving it away. Equally significant, they
invested large time blocks in the servanthood ideal of
Jesus as a satisfying way to develop a happy relationship
with time.

A Good Life or a Crowded Datebook

The famous family matriarch, Rose Kennedy, once
observed, "Crowding a life does not always enrich it."
She is right. Unnerving as it seems, an unexamined, frantic lifestyle feeds on itself to create a series of self-sus-
tained frustrations.

Often we fool ourselves into believing that outside
forces are responsible for our overfilled lives. For some
strange reason, blaming someone or some outside force
seems to end the discussion and free us from making any
adjustments. After all, this line of reasoning says, how
could we be responsible when we are victimized by the
expectations of others and helplessly out of breath? But
we *are* responsible.

To get life on track, start with a straightforward admission that clocks and calendars are helpful servants, not
uncontrollable slave drivers. To deal with these issues,
time questions must be asked: How can I make my life
count? What needs to be done? How can I do it? Who really
needs me?

More careful attention to intensity and urgency furnishes bold initiatives for cultivating this desired friendship with time. Robert S. Eliot's compelling questions help clarify the intensity and urgency concerns: If I knew I had only six months to live: (1) What would I have to do? (2) What would I want to do? and (3) What are the things I would neither have to do nor want to do?[4] Another approach is to evaluate each demand on our time by assigning it to one of three categories: trivial, important, or essential. Using either technique automatically forces introspection and evaluation, which help us choose what we really want to do with the priceless segments of our life called time. Remember, nothing is as momentous as it seems.

Like nourishing any relationship, developing a happy friendship with time requires reassignment of seconds, minutes, and days. Some time management authorities believe reassignment is difficult to achieve simply because only about 5 percent of our time is uncommitted. Therefore, before any new commitments are made, you must ask yourself what adjustments you are willing to make and what readjustments you can make. A half-hour investment in Bible reading requires thirty minutes taken away from another interest. A choice to spend an evening at home means that another commitment for the same night must be given up. Likewise, a two-day prayer retreat means forty-eight hours must be taken from something else. Bob Benson gave us direction for these realignments: "If you will ask God what He would do if it were His life, He would gladly tell you."[5]

Thus constant monitoring is needed to work toward a balanced life, even when priorities become temporarily blurred. Robert Wood's prayer sharpens distinctions between crowded schedules and fulfilled lives:

Almighty God, teach me timing . . .
There are times in my life to plant

an idea in the mind of an inquisitive child
a seed of hope for someone in need
the gift of trust in one birthing faith.
There are times in our lives
to scatter stones that build walls,
to gather stones that build bridges between individuals.
Teach us the times to seek
out the fellowship of the body of Christ,
the solitude of meditation,
to serve others with humility and love . . .[6]

Cloisters and Saints on the Run

Christian history shows us unnumbered pilgrims who withdrew to cloisters to live pious lives and gain control over the details of life. At the quiet place, they discovered the spiritual energy that enabled them to produce the literature of the inner life and to recuperate from shallow living. True to their satisfying discoveries, they recommend lengthy withdrawal from anything or anyone that drains us of spiritual vitality. Their advice feels good to us because all sojourners occasionally hunger for some facet of the cloistered life to slow their feverish pace and to fill their inner emptiness.

As radio commentator Paul Harvey would say, "Now for the rest of the story." What about those activists so involved in serving others that they never took time to write down their findings? One spiritual formation writer correctly observed: "Jesus was a holy man. There were times He had to be alone with the Father. But I am beginning to believe that His holiness did not come because He withdrew from life; He was holy because He entered into life at every level."[7] Could the reason we know so little about spiritual activists be the fact that they never found enough time to write and publish their insights and experiences?

Before activists are dismissed as unimportant or insignificant, we must consider how impoverished the world would be without all those superactive saints who dash through life with a prayer on their lips and a Bible in their hands. Examples are around us everywhere— some obvious, but others almost unnoticed. Patience Hole, pastor of the house-church of my childhood in Detroit, was a busy mother-in-Christ to her little flock— loving, caring for, and affirming us. Charles Hoos, while living in a hectic world like ours, functioned as both father and mother to his children, remodeled the church with his own hammer, baked birthday cakes, washed clothes, visited hospitals, demonstrated Christian compassion to the needy, and preached powerfully to human needs. Archie Woodward, evangelist and longtime family friend, kept a schedule that put him in such close touch with people that he was ready on a moment's notice to sing, pray, preach, play softball, or ride a motorcycle. J. V. Morsch, our pastor and friend during our first immediate family encounter with death, was and is a whirlwind for God. These active souls and thousands like them honed their spiritual growth on the anvil of selfless service for God and for their fellow human beings.

There can be no doubt that faith often prospers in the cloistered, withdrawn life with Christ, but God also travels busy roads with His activists. Maybe pioneer spiritual literature writers and more modern disciples put too much distance between action and contemplation. Maybe we do, too. A fulfilled life needs both. At certain periods withdrawal may be most needed, but at other times an exhilarating commitment to action is required.

In speaking of this balance, the Episcopal priest and theological educator James C. Fenhagen says of the apostle Paul, "His activism was the fruit of the relationship he enjoyed with the living Christ."[8] This interplay between thought and action builds on the fact that busy Marthas and meditative Marys are both needed and cherished in every life and in every generation.

Lived-out devotion is wonderfully nourished by a rhythm of solitude and service or waiting and doing. God shows himself in the crowded moments of our lives, but He appears in the quiet times, too. Catherine de Hueck Doherty calls us to aspire to both: "Because you are more aware of God, because you have been called to listen in your inner silence, you can bring God to the street, the party, the meeting, in a powerful way."[9] Consequently, there is no reason for believers to choose between reflection and action; both resource our aliveness, our usefulness, and our fulfillment. Meditation and prayer are the winds of God that drive the sails of spirituality to take us out into the deep places of adventuresome service and long-term satisfaction.[10]

Making Time for Faith Formation

Our perplexities about time change along with the transitions of our lives. Mothers-to-be think pregnancies will never end. Young parents wonder if babies will ever grow up. Middle-age couples long for grown children to come home more often. Cancer victims can't decide whether time moves too fast or too slow for them. Elderly people, with time to spare, long for more visits from friends. Nearly everyone, regardless of age or vocation, wishes to change the supply of time. Most people want more time, though a few want less, but such changes are not likely to happen. Since all this is true, the solution seems to be making better use of the time we already have. Think of the life-changing possibilities in a one-minute contact with God.

According to Carstens and Mahedy, "Many people find it surprisingly difficult to concentrate for a full minute on a single subject."[11] Amazing as it sounds, even when a month is available to consider a marriage proposal or a job change, no one spends all 43,200 minutes on that concern. Even when faced with serious choices, we only think about a specific issue for a few minutes several times a day. Therefore, Carstens and Mahedy conclude correctly, "Sound decisions or solutions to problems emerge from long stretches of intermittent consideration with the active part done about one minute at a time."[12]

The significance of this idea is obvious—we have more time available for decisions and faith formation than we think. Perhaps we have not allowed choice, love for a cause, or passion for a commitment to shape our time allocations enough.

Everyone has more frequent, short, time segments for growing a great soul than he or she thinks. My proposal to use fleeting time periods for spiritual development, however, is not new. The French spiritual pilgrim Fenelon suggested years ago: "We must often raise our heart to God. . . . All the most preoccupied moments are good times, even while eating and hearing others talk."[13] This concept shows God-seekers that street corners, quiet walks, fast freeways, and even long committee meetings give us time for encountering God.

Gear Up for Golden Moments

People easily forget routine happenings, but they sometimes remember epic moments forever. A contemporary author who understands life suggests, "If you throw your arms around such a moment and hug it like crazy, it may save your soul."[14] Everyone has at least one golden moment he or she never wants to forget. But each minute must be lived to the fullest to keep ready for these special experiences.

No one knows why a special moment happens when it does, and few of us are fully aware when we are making a memory. But the basic ingredient for creating these never-to-be-forgotten moments is time. For a small boy to build a soap box derby racing car for Cub Scouts means someone must invest time to show him how to use woodworking tools. For a college student with average ability to earn academic honors means a teacher invested large time commitments in her education. For salty sea breezes to blow through a crippled senior citizen's snow-white hair means someone coordinated the time-consuming logistics to get him on the houseboat. Every unforgettable experience means someone invested significant time commitments to make a special moment.

An unforgettable experience can sneak up on a parent talking with a little child. A glorious moment may show up as a surprising payoff for an apparently insignificant task done at church. Sometimes a dawn of meaning breaks in on an average day during a chance meeting of old friends. Tasting the passing moment fully, to borrow an idea from the French novelist Camus, may happen anytime or anywhere. Be ready for the memory of it, and be prepared to pay for a lovely moment by enjoying it.

God often sends these golden moments across faith formation bridges of worship, prayer, and service. Buechner makes the idea even more expansive: "In the final analysis, all moments are key moments, and life itself is grace."[15] Though momentous happenings cannot be orchestrated, they almost never happen without time commitments and active curiosity.

Golden moments are so delightful that no one wants to miss even one. To multiply the possibilities, James A. Michener advises, "Don't put off for tomorrow what you can do today, because if you enjoy it today you can do it again tomorrow."

I love the way author Robert J. Hastings tells us to keep ready for memorable moments: "Stop pacing the aisles and counting the miles. Instead, climb more mountains, eat more ice cream, go barefoot oftener, swim more rivers, watch more sunsets, laugh more, and cry less. Life must be lived as we go along."[16] The secret—savor each moment, search for its meaning, and hug the memory to your heart.

This openness required to relish golden moments shows in the devotional giant John Henry Jowett's prayer: "My Father, give me a sense of the unspeakable value of time. May I so live as to place a jewel in every moment."[17] The Sanskrit proverb tells us how:

> Look to this day
> For yesterday is only a dream,
> And tomorrow is only a vision,
> But today, well lived,
> Makes every yesterday a dream of happiness
> And every tomorrow a vision of hope.
> Look well, therefore, to this day.

Keep Committed to the Present

Though not thinking about spiritual development, former U.S. president Lyndon B. Johnson observed once that most of us put second things first. He is right; nobody knows why and nobody intends to do so. We just do. We focus on a long-gone past or an uncertain future while neglecting present possibilities. Such tendencies must be resisted. Scripture announces an important fact to aid us: "Jesus Christ is the same yesterday and today and forever" (Heb. 13:8). That fact makes every present moment special, useful, and redemptive.

Yet thousands allow themselves to be trapped, waiting for uncertain tomorrows or looking through rearview mirrors at life. Their regrets handcuff them to the past, while their fear about the future makes them hostage to problems that may never happen. Meanwhile, this life-squandering process squeezes significance out of today. Columnist Ann Landers explains the risk: "One of these days may be none of these days." She has the situation sized up accurately: the miracle of enjoying present blessings never happens without intentional vigilance.

To be present in the present may take more than a rational attempt to adjust the focus away from the past or the future. One remedy is to apply the Jesuit priest Jean de Caussade's enlightening phrase "sacrament of the present"[18] to all of life. We need to put out the welcome mat to the potential of the present. That word *sacrament* shines a clear light on making the present a good place to be and brings soul-stretching attitudes to mind— worshipful awe, a holy remembrance, a new start, an undeserved gift, a means of grace, or even a mystery from God. The knowledge that the present is a sacrament pushes us to seize the present so that we fill each moment with meaning. This sacramental notion also graphically reminds us of something we already know— that God stands ready to infuse the present moment with more potential than we can imagine. Then life need not feel like an empty cup, a dead-end street, or a barren wilderness.

Cherishing the present adds zest to our spiritual journey. Writing in the autumn of life, Sarah Patton-Boyle explains the rewards of refocusing on the present: "The world around me began to sparkle and shine. I perceived sunlight in a different way. Flowers, trees, clouds, the richly varied music of nature and of man rounded out and became full. In my marrow and muscle, I felt the sometimes hastening, sometimes plodding energy of all living things."[19] For our own good, we must resist living in the future or making the past a deadly shrine. Celebrate the present for its possibilities and grace; that will fill tomorrow's memories about today full of peace.

In small, significant ways we carry imprints of every day on our memories wherever we go and whatever we do. Though few realize it, each unlived day irrevocably undermines the future in some way, even as each kindly deed enriches every tomorrow. Clearly, if we are to make friends with time, Paul's teaching must be heeded in the present: "Take time and trouble to keep yourself spiritually fit" (1 Tim. 4:7, Phillips).

Guidance for joyous living in the present tense shines through this anonymous poem:

> Today is ours—let's live it.
> And love is strong—let's give it.
> A song can help—let's sing it.
> A peace is dear—let's bring it.
> The past is gone—don't rue it.
> Our work is here—let's do it.
> The world is wrong—let's right it.
> If evil comes—let's fight it.
> The road is rough—let's clear it.
> The future vast—don't fear it.
> Is faith asleep—let's wake it.
> Today is free—let's take it.

To enjoy a satisfying life, make the most of all three time dimensions—past, present, future—by allowing God to inform your present from the past and to nourish today with hopes about tomorrow. A fulfilled life depends on an adventuresome attitude toward time. Find ways to make time your best friend.

Making Time Your Friend

"Hurry sickness" can be healed, chains of frenzied deadlines can be broken, and a friendly relationship with time can be developed. One starts by mobilizing one's own will and priorities. But how? How can we, when we have the same number of hours as everyone else, make our lives less hectic and more fulfilled? What constructive strategies can we use?

1. Let done be done. Leave a finished assignment. Additional work on a completed project increases frustration. Charlie Shedd reports a young career woman's self-discovery: "No wonder I'm worn out! I do everything I do so many times. First I worry about doing it—then when I have done it, I do it over, worrying whether I did it right." She can teach us something important: give a task your best and trust the rest to God. Only the Father knows the long-term results of a deed, but He knows.

2. Boss your time. Scrutinize your schedule to see what your calendar says about your priorities. Does your datebook support what you really consider to be important? A dedicated cardiac surgeon places patient care ahead of golf. A serious law student considers preparation for her bar exam more important than shopping. A committed critical-care nurse is more eager to ease suffering than to complete insurance forms. An effective teacher prefers sharpening a student's mind over leaving school early each afternoon. And some executives are voluntarily downshifting in corporate life to have more time for family and for themselves. Try bossing your time so you can be more efficient and more fulfilled.

Greater time control can be achieved by a more flexible approach to scheduling. One time management expert recommends allowing 25 percent more time for each task than you expect it to take; the cushion allows additional time for each task or provides free time if the extra time is not needed. Another specialist suggests that no more than half of our time should be scheduled, so that we allow for interruptions, unplanned demands, or creative thought. Sadly, but not surprisingly, schedules often reveal something significantly different from the way their owners planned to use their lives.

Critically question your calendar. Quiz your datebook to learn whether your priorities control your actions. Accept the fact that an excuse of busyness often keeps you from finishing difficult assignments or making hard decisions. Just as a checkbook assigns values to spending, a datebook assigns values to conduct.

Why not refocus your activities on what really matters? Don't rush your life away.

3. Shun the success trap. The road to the top can make you miserable. Success seldom satisfies for long; the thing we most want often brings undesirable burdens. Fast-lane living frequently traps people in unsatisfying success and leaves little time for spiritual growth.

Many individuals, by the time they reach middle age (or even before), feel locked into a professional or corporate wilderness. Regrettably, the same possibility of overreaching ambitions exists for blue-collar workers and small-business owners. To avoid this trap, try evaluating your intentions against every unrelenting deadline, every desire for prominence, and every hunger for instant gratification. Are you paying too much for success?

A fulfilled life requires a balance of reflection and activity. Why not try to fire up as much enthusiasm for interior development, prayer, and encounter with Scripture as you already feel for security, work, or hobbies? Then at the end of the day, quiet your body, center your mind, and talk with God. Surprisingly, the day's stress will ease as adventures in prayer, Scripture reading, and meditation increase.

4. Apply disciplines to the demands of your life. Like sips of refreshing cool water, the spiritual disciplines can be used when you run into pressing time constraints. As needed, Christ makes encouragement and a sense of His nearness available to us in one-minute segments.

Even though the spiritual disciplines are as old as Christianity, the well-known practices of fasting, sharing, prayer, and serious study of Scripture are useful ways to deal with the pressures of modern life. But these traditional disciplines must be infused with meaning to avoid the cartoon character Ziggy's testimony, "Lately I've gotten into transcendental vegetation."

Ask yourself several useful questions: What insights about the use of time do I receive from Scripture? What ideas for uncluttering my life come to me as I pray? How can intercession and centering on Christ lessen my time pressures? What can I do to make tomorrow and next week spiritually significant?

5. Develop a time log. A time log will help you keep track of time and audit the results; it also helps an individual acknowledge ownership of time and control its use. As an effective way to evaluate priorities, try keeping an activity log in fifteen-minute segments for a week or a month, using only categories that make sense to you, such as family, job, leisure, television viewing, devotional development, and worship.

Try holding yourself accountable for what really matters to you. Admit that your use of time ultimately determines the kind of life you live. Wasting time is wasting life. Schedule time when you can withdraw for a change of activity, geography, and people.

6. Learn to say no. Say no for the right reasons. Sometimes we can't resist accepting too many commitments because the requests flatter us. But no one can do everything everyone wants them to do. To cultivate your inner life, some worthy tasks must wait for another day or be done by somebody else. Saying no makes room in your schedule to prepare for a future task or to nourish your soul.

Then, too, overcommitments often result in inferior work. Elton Trueblood was right, "Holy shoddy is still shoddy." When we overcommit ourselves, the quality of our service suffers, the Kingdom is weakened, and we no longer strive for excellence. Rightly used, saying no helps us pay closer attention to the meaning of our life.

7. Drop "too busy" from your conversation. God never overloads anyone, even though others may place too many demands on us or we may overcommit ourselves. When tempted to say "too busy," ask yourself if God has given you too much to do or if He has given you less time than others. The Father's pace always produces worthy accomplishments and fulfilling satisfaction. And He is never impressed with a frenzied lifestyle—even that of His more pious children. Self-centered motivation, overcommitment, poor organization, or inappropriate priorities are usually the real culprits.

Try listening to, and then personally avoiding, the absurd things others say about time. Notice how some people talk about being busy, but in the next sentence discuss watching television for hours. Or they may discuss the crushing time demands of their job, but brag the next moment about long coffee breaks. Consider that your conversations may sound just as amusing to others. Drop those words "too busy" from your vocabulary and harmonize your day around the way God wants you to use your time.

8. Hurry up to slow down. Accelerate routine activities to finish necessities more quickly. Iron faster so that you can read more slowly. Hurry grocery shopping so that you can pray more leisurely. Wash your car quickly so that you can take a walk or explore nature with a child. Step lively as you mow the lawn so that you can have

more time for Scripture. Rush newspaper reading so that
you can take a drive to view a spectacular sunset.

Hurry routine responsibilities so that you can develop
godliness in a more methodical manner. Pace yourself.
What can be speeded up? What can be eliminated? What
needs more attention? Spiritual growth usually requires
a reappropriation of available time.

9. Measure life by quality. Stop judging your life by
how many customers, clients, accounts, committees, or
jobs you hold in the church. Consider the comment by
Will Rogers: "It's not so much what you do each day—
it's what you get *done* that counts." Since there is so much
to be enjoyed on days that are not ruled by the clock,
why not take off your watch on a weekend or holiday to
allow yourself to be directed by your natural sense of
time? John Gardner suggests favored places and activities for quality life development, such as a walk at the
beach or a special fishing stream, or a nonverbal pastime
such as music, gardening, sports, light reading, or work
with one's hands.[20]

Begin by cherishing quality relationships and achievements; then rid your schedule of commitments that only
feed your vanity. Take time to get better acquainted with
your family. Assign yourself time to cultivate your inner
world. Try something new to develop a growing edge—
a new sport, a class, or a hobby. Ask God to cure your
hurry sickness so that you can enjoy life more.

10. Use Jesus as a model for time evaluation. Jesus
showed us how the road to spirituality is always under
construction, and He provides us with a magnificent
example of how to use hours and days to build a fulfilled
life. Remember the renewal Jesus received from regular
withdrawal from His ordinary routines.

Compare the way you use your time with the way Jesus
used His. Ask yourself at the beginning of the day how
many hours you are willing to place in God's hands for

Him to use as He chooses. Adjust your commitments to what He wants done. How does God evaluate the way you used yesterday? What does He think about your plans for tomorrow? Be as specific as possible because vagueness can be confusing and deadly.

As you consider how you can make a friend of time, try using as your own the petition Jesus prayed, "Father, into your hands I commit my spirit" (Luke 23:46). Ask God to help you develop a friendly relationship with time so that you may experience strength instead of weakness, peace instead of frustration, and confidence instead of tension. Flavia, the greeting card designer, says it so well: "Do something wonderful with this day—for it will never come again."

Exercises to Get Your Soul in Shape

- Let done be done.
- Boss your time.
- Shun the success trap.
- Apply disciplines to the demands of your life.
- Develop a time log.
- Learn to say no.
- Drop "too busy" from your conversation.
- Hurry up to slow down.
- Measure life by quality.
- Use Jesus as a model for time evaluation.

**His powerful Word is sharp as
a surgeon's scalpel, cutting
through everything, whether doubt
or defense, laying us open
to listen and obey.
Nothing and no one is impervious
to God's Word. We can't get
away from it—no matter what.**

Hebrews 4:12–13

(TM)

છ૭

Almighty God—Inspirer
of the Holy Book

Invade and enrich my routines with refreshing,
commanding, compelling insights from Scripture.
Ground me in Your ways and familiarize me with
Your will. Teach me to be at home in Your Word.

Empower me to love and live the Bible as
   inspiration for a holy walk,
   instruction for continual obedience,
   guidance for righteousness,
   sustenance from One who loves me most.

(Complete this prayer for yourself.)

Apply Your Word to my life to help me
   make sense of my ambiguities including . . .
   make me like Christ in these situations . . .
   sharpen my efforts in these circumstances . . .
Thank you for the molding power of Your Word.
   Amen.

Follow the Manufacturer's Manual

A Blueprint for Growing a Great Soul

> Our house crashes in ruins because it is not founded on the word of Jesus Christ.
> —*Dietrich Bonhoeffer*

An eager teenager sounded like an ideal buyer when he phoned about a Toyota I had advertised in the newspaper. He was searching for his first car, to be a sixteenth-birthday gift from his mother. In spite of mileage and age, our sporty Celica was well maintained because we had faithfully followed the manufacturer's manual.

Within an hour after his phone call, my young friend brought his mother, an ambitious advertising executive, and his best buddy to check out the car. He expressed delight with the Celica's condition and equipment, which included a five-speed transmission, sporty wheels, a flashy paint job, a top-of-the-line stereo, and an equalizer. He announced with utter amazement on the test drive, "Mom, everything works." In no time, mother and son huddled on my front porch for a conference and decided to buy the car. After we settled on a price, his mother wrote a deposit check, and we agreed to transfer the title. They would take delivery the next day. All of this produced tantalizing excitement for this high school buyer and assured me that my car would have a good home.

On the spur of the moment, I loaned him the manufacturer's manual until the next day, when it would be his. And I am glad I did.

When they returned the following day, I was astonished at how much this inquisitive teenager had taught himself overnight about my Celica. As he slid under the wheel, he knew the location and operation of every system. Motivated by anticipation, he had mastered many details from the manufacturer's manual. He had discovered that the car's manual provided information about how to make automobile ownership trouble-free and even enjoyable. He learned how fast a Toyota should be driven in each gear, and he found answers to his questions about tire pressure, fuses, and tune-ups. The manufacturer's manual suggested fine points on how to care for the Toyota even after the owner became familiar with the car.

The Bible, the Manufacturer's Manual for spiritual development, does the same for us by giving instructions on how to live a quality life. Scripture, though not intended as an authority on science or history, provides truth about God and offers insights for making sense out of the puzzling aspects of the human pilgrimage. The Manufacturer's Manual contains amazingly useful guidance for inner wellness and a happy adjustment to life.

A skilled technician who loved the Bible because it resourced his living so well was hired to repair a giant telescope. The chief astronomer discovered the repairman reading his Bible during a lunch break. The scientist scoffed, "What good do you expect to get from the Bible? It's hopelessly out of date, and you don't even know who wrote it."

After a thoughtful pause, the puzzled repairman inquired, "Do you use the multiplication table around this place? Do you know who wrote it?"

Quickly the scientist replied, "We use the multiplication table. We don't know who wrote it, but we do know it works. It always works."

"That's why I trust the Bible," the repairman replied. "It works."

A Startlingly Unique Book

The Bible works for those who seriously try to understand its message, and it helps readers discover their reason for being. Nothing in the world is as significant to the seeker after God as the day Scripture seizes him, so that the Bible belongs to him and he belongs to the Bible. This happens when readers allow the Bible to speak to their sacred inner center. Like no other literature, its resources are as essential to life as oxygen, water, and food.

Inasmuch as the Bible deals with both daily experiences and ultimate life-and-death issues, it authoritatively and dynamically challenges every reader, including beginners and veterans, students and scholars, young and old, simple and sophisticated, common folks and kings. Designed and preserved by the Father, this faithful Book nourishes our souls, inspires our minds, and energizes our wills. It tells us more than we could otherwise know about God, life, and ourselves.

The fact that the Bible is so relevant to life surprises many first-time readers and keeps astonishing even more frequent readers. It is amazingly up-to-date. Holy Scripture—as a road map out of the complexities of nonfulfillment, frustration, and moral confusion—explains how God intends life to function. It deals with the cost and consequences of being, doing, and having.

Apparently many moderns think about God only with a mild intellectual curiosity. Perhaps they have not needed the Bible because they have never experienced anguish of soul resulting from sorrow, ambiguity, or sin. Or maybe they have never felt perplexed by destructive disappointment or bruised by painful loss. But they will. And when devastating circumstances force them to take a serious interest in God, the Bible stands ready with strength for the soul.

An Incredibly Influential Book

Even in contemporary culture, the Bible still has far-reaching influence and surprising impact. Though secularization has clearly infiltrated Western civilization, Scripture still affects modern society. Our language and literature are packed so full of biblical words, phrases, and ideals that no one can talk or think about the basics of life for long without dealing with scriptural ideas. Even secular fields of inquiry like psychology, history, and sociology keep rediscovering that the teachings of Scripture are as true to human experience as studies in their own disciplines.

The Bible influences individuals, too. This means that an obedient hearing of Scripture settles many confusions because the Bible calibrates faith with human experience. This potential is underscored by Paul Scherer: "The comfort of the Scriptures never was intended to soothe you or make you feel right, never mind how nasty you've been, or how terrible things are. Rather, it was intended to send you back into the fight, whatever yours happens to be, with all the reinforcements God Almighty himself can throw in."[1] That is exactly what the Bible does when it opens windows of reality and helps us deal with both the bumps and the near-fatal wrecks of the fast track. Scripture calls us to replace stress caused by self-sovereignty with God-centered living.

A Lovers' Quarrel Book

Though it is not realistic to expect that any single view about the Bible will be acceptable to everyone, various debates might be viewed as a kind of lovers' quarrel intended to clarify the purpose and meaning of Scripture. Of course, some take the Bible's authority more seriously than others, but anyone who studies Scripture for whatever reason and with whatever motive finds that the Bible judges its readers rather than being judged by them.

Maybe these debates finally boil down to expressions of abiding affection, perhaps even respect, for the influence the Bible has had on the development of civilization, culture, and personal character. The important reality is that when Scripture is seriously applied to life, it transforms individuals and calls civilizations to righteousness. The Bible continues, as it always has, to nourish the soul and reduce anxious tensions.

After all the profound arguments are finished and the impressive research is published, simple believers, sophisticated scholars, and everyone in between find a wonderful quality of life when they heed the message of Scripture and follow this amazing book to Christ, its central character. Reading the Bible helps us know Jesus better. In profoundly significant ways, the Bible changes those who read it, who listen to it, who meditate on it day and night, and who apply it to the details of life.

Legend says when Charles Spurgeon was criticized for not defending the Bible, he humorously replied, "Defend the Bible! I would as soon think of defending a lion. Unchain the Bible, and it will defend itself." At another time and in a different setting, U.S. President Woodrow Wilson explained the far-reaching influence of Scripture: "Give the Bible to the people, unadulterated, pure, unaltered, unexplained, uncheapened, and then see it work through the whole nature." And thousands of years before Spurgeon or Wilson, Jeremiah affectionately announced, "Thy words were found, and I did eat them; and thy word was unto me the joy and rejoicing of mine heart" (Jer. 15:16, KJV). Spurgeon, Wilson, and Jeremiah all agreed that the Bible needs application, rather than defense. Scripture transforms individuals, families, and even civilizations.

An Enduring Book

Written over a fifteen-hundred-year time span by approximately forty authors, the Bible stands as the most enduring book in the history of literature. In spite of this long period of writing, the Bible as a library of sixty-six books possesses an unprecedented unity not found in other literary collections. To people of every generation for two thousand years, this miraculous book has communicated God's provisions to make persons holy, useful, and happy. Its uniquely eye-opening characteristics include unity of thought and enormous personal impact.

Any record of the Bible's longevity shows it has survived fire, apathy, skeptics, disuse, and the recopying efforts of hundreds of scribes. Divine preservation can be observed in its mind-stretchingly accurate transmission, which can be seen by comparing present copies of Scripture with hand-copied manuscripts written before the printing press was invented. This remarkably reliable record gives contemporary people the assurance that God continues to speak through Scripture to the human dilemma.

Centuries have tested the validity of the Bible's message, and history records how it has redemptively affected millions. The biographies of the saints demonstrate how Scripture decreases anxiety when applied with submissive expectancy to the pressing issues of life. Coming to the Bible always provides personal spiritual benefit when the readers pray with the Psalmist, "Open my eyes that I may see wonderful things in your law" (119:18). Now, as always, Scripture illuminates darkness in the soul and lightens burdens in the mind. Its long-time endurance is remarkable, and its abiding influence is incredible.

A Soul Food Book

In many congregations on an average Sunday morning, Scripture offers a staggering range of help for human need, including judgment for ethical issues, comfort for pain, clarity for confusion, inspiration for despair, and discipline for rebellion. William Johnston is right: "The force and power of the Word of God is so great that it remains the support and energy of the church, the strength of faith for her children, the food for the soul, and the pure and perennial source of spiritual life."[2] And there is more. All across the world in more private settings, as thousands of individual readers and study groups apply its teachings to their situations, the Bible heals the desperate emotional turmoil and spiritual wounds so common to so many lives.

Once I had the good fortune to serve as pastor to a congregation whose style and perspectives meshed with mine wonderfully. One Sunday I preached that the Bible was God's Love Letter to serious spiritual pilgrims who read, digested, and practiced its teachings. Though the sermon could have used more polish, a sense of God's nearness pervaded the sanctuary and elevated all who were part of the worshiping community. During the following week, I received an affirming note from Frances Tullin, one who possesses the lovely gift of encouragement. Part of her letter captured the exact effect Scripture was intended to have on us: "Henceforth, when I open my Bible, I'm sure it will be with a sense of holy hush. May my response always include loving obedience and joyful slavery to Scripture." Frances discovered and summarized several desirable outcomes from the study of Scripture: holy hush quiets the heart in worship, loving obedience makes one eager to follow divine guidance, and joyful slavery sounds like a synonym for wholehearted devotion. That is what diligent readers encounter in Scripture to enable them to be genuinely Christian in all things.

Though evidence abounds that the Bible is no longer read as frequently as it once was, it continues to be a readily accessible resource for contemporary people. The Good Book continues as a best-seller: $170 million was spent for Bibles in the United States in a recent year; and the Gideons place one million copies each year in hotels, motels, and hospitals. A few years ago, six new translations were published in one twelve-month period, and *Books in Print* listed fifty-five pages of Bible-related entries, as compared with fifteen pages about food and fourteen pages related to sex.[3] Copies of Scripture are available everywhere. Nearly everyone in the Western world owns a copy of the Bible or knows where to find one.

However, digesting and practicing the Bible depends on use, not accessibility. A copy of Scripture on every bookshelf is not enough. The Bible must be read if one is to hear the voice of God, get to know Jesus better, and learn how to live. Therefore, the Bible must be picked up and read. It must be loved and lived.

A Stress-Reducing Book

Paul wrote these convincing words in a letter to his friends at Rome: "For everything that was written in the past was written to teach us, so that through endurance and the encouragement of the Scriptures we might have hope" (Rom. 15:4). In one short sentence, the apostle underscores the power of Scripture to instruct us, to resource steadfastness, and to inspire hope. Everyone I know needs all three—instruction, enablement, and inspiration.

Even when the Bible is put to tough tests, it makes good on Paul's promises with soul-stirring guidance that takes the stress out of our bewildering complexities and breaks the grip of our anxieties. Scripture supplies us with strength so that we can deal with the whirling vortex of tension-related problems. Note the ancient, though ever contemporary promises.

As a *relief for loneliness*, Scripture pledges:

"Be strong and of good courage, fear not, nor be afraid of them: for the Lord thy God, he it is that doth go with thee; he will not fail thee, nor forsake thee" (Deut. 31:6, KJV).

For *frightening fears*, the Bible promises:

"Peace I leave with you, my peace I give unto you: not as the world giveth, give I unto you. Let not your heart be troubled, neither let it be afraid" (John 14:27, KJV).

As an *antidote for anger*, the Word of God instructs:

For if you forgive men when they sin against you, your heavenly Father will also forgive you" (Matt. 6:14).

As a *help for frustration,* the Bible guarantees:

"Trust in the Lord with all your heart and lean not on your own understanding; in all your ways acknowledge him, and he will make your paths straight" (Prov. 3:5–6).

"But they that wait upon the Lord shall renew their strength; they shall mount up with wings as eagles; they shall run, and not be weary; and they shall walk, and not faint" (Isa. 40:31, KJV).

As a *strength in suffering*, Scripture promises:

"I consider that our present sufferings are not worth comparing with the glory that will be revealed in us" (Rom. 8:18).

"Weeping may remain for a night, but rejoicing comes in the morning" (Ps. 30:5).

As a *defense for discouragement*, the Word of God provides:

"Do not be anxious about anything, but in everything by prayer and petition with thanksgiving, present your requests to God. And the peace of God, which transcends all understanding, will guard your hearts and your minds in Christ Jesus" (Phil. 4:6–7).

As an *encouragement during illness,* the Bible assures us:

"He forgives all my sins and heals all my diseases; he redeems my life from the pit and crowns me with love and compassion. He satisfies my desires with good things, so that my youth is renewed like the eagle's" (Ps. 103:3–5).

And in *periods of bereavement*, the Scriptures say:

"Yea, though I walk through the valley of the shadow of death, I will fear no evil: for thou art with me; thy rod and thy staff they comfort me" (Ps. 23:4, KJV).

Jesus said to her, "I am the resurrection and the life. He who believes in me will live, even though he dies" (John 11:25).

These timeless promises offer lifesaving assurances to people who live in a secular world where everything seems to be coming loose from its foundations. Author John Jay Chapman explains the stabilizing capability of Scripture: "The Bible is a cloud by day and a pillar of fire by night, and the darker the skies grow, whether above an epoch or an individual, the more light it emits." Scripture alleviates anxiety because it deals with essential, bedrock, changeless issues. As a Word-informed veteran of the way attested, "It is truly true." This grand old Book stands true in the contemporary world with enablement for our most difficult needs. The Bible has one encompassing message: human beings have problems, but God provides miraculous cures.

A Quality-Living Book

Scripture awakens and satisfies longings in the soul for God. The Bible, as the main communication channel between God and man, takes us to Christ, who offers comfort for bereavement, rebuke for sin, reenergization for attaining forgotten goals, warning against rebellion, and relief from stress. As an objective written record, it saves God-seekers from a tidal wave of private notions about spirituality.

The Bible is a surprisingly simple book, even though there are some hard-to-understand passages in it. Some readers are unnecessarily intimidated when their preacher mentions Greek and Hebrew, the original languages of the Scripture. Others wonder how difficult the Bible may be for them when they start reading complicated passages like those in Revelation. But anyone, regardless of experience or education, can understand enough of the Bible to discover a new quality of life in relationship with Jesus Christ. The Bible, therefore, continues to be a confusing book only to those who do not open its pages.

Conversely, because the riches of Scripture are so inexhaustible, lifelong Bible readers, students, and scholars discover something new each time they read. In both simple and profound ways, the Bible helps readers get better acquainted with Christ as the living Lord speaks through Scripture. Long ago Jesus explained His relatedness to Scripture to the Pharisees, "You search the scriptures, because you think that in them you have eternal life; and *it is they that bear witness to me*; yet you refuse to come to me that you may have life" (John 5:39–40, RSV, italics added).

The written Word, the Bible, takes us to Jesus, the living Word; then God's message flows through paper and ink to help us become intimately acquainted with Christ. The eye-opening implications of this idea are expressed in Frank Laubach's astounding statement that "nine-tenths of the human race would follow Christ if they knew who He is, when they will not follow an abstract truth."[4] That is what the Bible does; it introduces us to Jesus, so that He becomes a living person for us rather than a theoretical notion or abstract ideal.

The life and teachings of Jesus connect the Old and New Testaments. Taken alone, the Old Testament is an incomplete book that looks forward to Christ. Likewise, the New Testament record of the life of Jesus cannot be understood without its Old Testament roots. This interface between Jesus and the Bible is well expressed in Buechner's extraordinary sentence, "I wanted to learn about Christ—about the Old Testament, which had been His Bible, and the New Testament, which was the Bible about Him."[5] This interdependence becomes abundantly clear in the first chapter of Matthew and continues through many direct Old Testament quotations in the New Testament: Bible authorities teach that

more than thirteen hundred Old Testament references
and allusions can be found in the New Testament. Thus
the Old Testament forms the foundation for the New
Testament, even as the New Testament completes the
Old Testament.

The Bible guides seekers into holy, happy, useful living—God's strategy for inner wholeness. Paul wrote to
Timothy, his son in the ministry, "From infancy you have
known the holy Scriptures, *which are able to make you
wise for salvation through faith in Christ Jesus"* (2 Tim. 3:15,
italics added). The Psalmist led Old Testament congregations in singing, "How can a young man keep his way
pure? *By living according to your word"* (119:9, italics
added). The ancient hymn writer of the Psalms continued, "I have hidden your word in my heart *that I might
not sin against you"* (v. 11, italics added). The Bible claims
to be a source for holistic living: "All scripture is given
by inspiration of God, and is *profitable for doctrine, for
reproof, for correction, for instruction in righteousness*: That
the man of God may be perfect, thoroughly furnished
unto all good works" (2 Tim. 3:16–17, KJV, italics added).
According to this record, God's prescribed path to wholeness is inner purity.

The Bible, as a source book for healing stress, makes
us see ourselves as we actually are. Hebrews 4:12 says,
"The word of God is quick, and powerful, and sharper
than any two-edged sword, piercing even to the dividing
asunder of soul and spirit, and of the joints and marrow,
and is a *discerner of the thoughts and intents of the heart"*
(KJV, italics added). But seekers after God need not be
frightened by this new self-awareness because the Bible
also shows them how to close the gap between who they
are and who they can become. The Bible helps eliminate
the tension between being and becoming by making both
possible and enjoyable. From Scripture, the serious

seeker finds the path to a quality life; then serenity replaces stress.

A Demanding Book

Many people find the Bible stifling and boring. This happens because they read an occasional fragment for tradition's sake, though they prefer novels, newspapers, magazines, or television. At the other end of the spectrum, some insist they must have frequent contact with the Bible because for them, it is a fascinatingly helpful book that speaks to their emotional, intellectual, and spiritual concerns. Obedient yieldedness makes the difference even if the Bible's truth is uncomfortable.

Though other books can be read at whatever level of intensity the reader chooses for instruction, information, or pleasure, this Book pressures individuals to master its message. Precisely at this point, the Bible is significantly different from all other books because it renews and enriches only those who read with a yielded *yes*. Nothing is more vital to the ability to understand Scripture than wholehearted devotion to Christ. When out of tune with God, the inner world is cluttered with self-centered sin, harbored resentments, and neglected spiritual opportunities. In contrast, a clean inner life sharpens one's ability to hear the message of Scripture so that one can escape the enslavement of "what is" to move on to the point of "what can be." Useful techniques allow the Bible to nourish the inner world.

Start simply. Beginners should think of the Bible as a library of books, so a reader need not commence at Genesis and read through to Revelation. At the outset of a spiritual quest, it is useful to browse through this sixty-six-book library until a section captures one's interest and speaks to one's need. A plan for those who are new to Scripture might be to begin with Matthew 5–7 (the Sermon on the Mount); Psalms 23, 24, 100, 122, 139; Isaiah 35, 55; the Gospels of Mark and Luke; or Paul's letter to the Philippians. Next, begin cultivating a friendship with Old Testament prophets like Jeremiah, Amos, Hosea, or Micah. Then turn to the Acts of the Apostles in the New Testament for exciting accounts of the early church. After completing these sections, the reader will be ready for almost any passage.

Take time. History records stalwart saints who arose as early as four o'clock in the morning to read Scripture. Others read all night. Though their examples do not offer precise patterns for today, they do demonstrate that spiritual development requires us to take quality time for Bible reading. It is time well spent because every relationship and responsibility goes better after we have saturated our minds and souls with God's point of view and expectations.

It is more desirable to invest fifteen quality minutes per day than to wait to have longer, sporadic time blocks for study. Why not move past yesterday's failures in Bible reading and begin a vital relationship with the Holy Book now? Free yourself from the patterns others suggest to develop a workable method of your own.

Read with anticipation. To counteract boredom, count on receiving a fresh word from God each time you read. Anticipation nourishes readiness to listen and learn. Persons who look for a fresh word from Scripture are seldom disappointed. Receptivity always expands as new truth is allowed into the shady nooks and obscure corners of life. Those who expect the Bible to speak to their situation usually discover a gold mind of resources.

Read in spite of feelings. Everyone has mood swings that fluctuate for no apparent reason. To keep from being victimized by moods, individuals should read the Bible when they feel like it, read when they don't feel like it, and read when they have no feelings at all. How encouraging during "down moods" to read the Psalm, "My soul is weary with sorrow; strengthen me according to your word" (119:28).

Read for meanings. The Bible is a letter from the Enlightener who knows everything. Thus, the God-seeker should read the Bible until it says something significant to him. While it may seem desirable to read ten verses, two chapters, or a whole book at one sitting, it is generally more rewarding to read until the Bible speaks to your current situation. Stop and listen to key words, phrases, verses, or paragraphs; a meeting of meanings is more important than any prescribed procedure or set strategy.

Keep reading in spite of difficult passages. Follow Spurgeon's advice when you come to a puzzling passage: "When I am eating fish and come upon a bone, I don't fling the whole fish away. I put the bone on the side of the plate so that I can go on enjoying the fish." Take time to seek clarification from commentaries, atlases, dictionaries, and other study aids. But keep reading. Think of Scripture as God's personal word to you for each new day.

Share it. One gifted Bible teacher said, "It was by teaching that I learned what I know about the Bible." Home Bible studies, family devotions, Bible classes, and even casual conversation offer opportunities to encourage others with Scripture. A shared word from the Bible frequently relieves personal perplexity. To offer a promise from Scripture provides a lift for the giver and keeps the receiver thinking about the passage for a long time, so both are energized by its message.

To encourage lifelong growth, remember two characteristics of Scripture that stand forever: the Bible is simple enough that anyone can find the way to God and challenging enough to stimulate the most brilliant mind.

How to Use the Bible to Enrich Life

The Bible, a living, two-thousand-year-old book, is the most useful resource for quality living available to the human family. It will continue to serve as a promise of God's faithfulness as long as people remain on earth. Like the brilliant college freshman who knows everything until he meets a wise old person who tells him how life really works, Scripture keeps amazing folks. It is full of wisdom and truth to help readers deal with life as it is. Let's consider several ways to maximize these benefits.

1. Personalize a passage. Read until you receive a word that speaks to your situation. Put your name in the promise as you read: "I will never leave {your name} nor forsake {your name}" (Heb. 13:5, KJV). "Who shall separate {your name} from the love of Christ? shall trouble or hardship or persecution or famine or nakedness or danger or sword?" (Rom. 8:35). "I will not leave {your name} as orphans; I will come to {your name}" (John 14:18).

Personalize a passage by allowing it to take you to Jesus. This can be done by reading what our Lord did or said in the Gospels. Then contrast what you do and say in similar circumstances. Few experiences are so humbling, but it provides healing medicine for complacency or selfishness.

Another way to make Scripture your own is to pray it back to God. On your knees, with your Bible open to a passage, simply pray, "Lord, I think this passage promises help for my present problem." Or, "Lord, this passage makes demands I cannot meet. I need Your help now." Or, "Lord, open the meaning of this passage for me. Overcome my slow mind and active resistance. I want the mind of Christ." This method harmonizes belief with behavior as a reader moves from merely reading the Bible to actually living it.

2. Enter Scripture as an active participant. Look at a miracle, an event, a parable, a relationship, or even a single word through the eyes of the people who were there. Allow its first meaning to take root in you. Seek to apply all your senses to help you live the experience and listen for its contemporary significance. How did Lazarus feel as he threw off his graveclothes? What would it be like to spend time with Peter and John? As you read Jeremiah, think how troubled his times seemed to him. How would it feel to be in prison with Paul? Or, what was the leper's reaction when Jesus healed him?

For example, in your mind, climb into the tree with Zacchaeus to get a better view of Jesus. Try to imagine every detail of that event. See, hear, and smell the pressing crowd. Feel the burning heat. Grip the tree limb. Sneeze in the swirling dust. Then, allow your heart to melt with devotion as Jesus calls your name and invites himself to your home. Be an active participant who views the incident as if it happened yesterday or this morning.

3. Develop a personal Bible study method. Find a method that works well for you. The SMA method, both simple and useful, unlocks a passage with three questions: What does it *say*? What does it *mean*? How can it be *applied* to life? (S = say; M = mean; A = apply.)

A second technique uses three dimensions. *Then* (exegesis) asks what the original writer meant when the passage was first written; *always* (exposition) asks what truth in this passage applies to human situations in every age; and *now* (application) asks what the passage says to your own situation. That trio—then, always, and now—can be counted on to open the meaning of the Bible.

Another helpful approach is to follow Terry Hall's suggestion that people write a short summary title for each chapter of Scripture in their own study Bibles. His guidelines for labeling each chapter are: (1) Use four words or less, (2) discover the original thought of the writer, (3) consider the chapter's uniqueness, and (4) retain the big idea.[6] This approach allows readers to relate each chapter to their lives, consider how the paragraphs fit together, and summarize the chapter's meaning. It also provides a study guide for subsequent readings.

Effective Bible study begins with the assumption that the paragraph is the basic study unit that deals with one central idea. These sections, marked with a paragraph symbol in the King James Version, have regular paragraph indentations in newer translations. Though there are many powerful single verses, to study each passage in the context of a paragraph, chapter, or entire book deepens understanding.

4. Participate seriously in biblical preaching. Accurate hearing of a sermon is as important as preaching a sermon. The communication process is like the sound of a tree falling in a remote forest; while it can be argued that the falling tree made a crashing sound, nothing was communicated if no one heard. In the same way, preaching must be heard to be effective. Wholehearted participation by the listener requires serious mental, emotional, and spiritual engagement with the biblical passage, the preacher's thoughts, and the implications of the sermon.

Why not consider sermons as a source to help you better understand Scripture? Persons who attend worship services every Sunday morning receive twenty-six hours of Bible teaching each year (fifty-two sermons times thirty minutes of preaching); those who attend an additional service each week double the impact. Think of the possibilities of personal spiritual growth when one experiences fifty-two hours of biblical instruction each year for a lifetime. In this way, the promise that faith comes by hearing (Rom. 10:17) becomes an actuality, and special blessing is promised to those who read, hear, and heed (Rev. 1:3).

This kind of sermon hearing, much more than courteous listening, requires tough mental engagement with the biblical content of the sermon while it is being preached and long after it is finished. Since the sermon preached and the sermon heard are never identical, the listener may go back to Scripture to check meanings. A clarification might even be requested from the preacher; he will be gratified to know someone gave his sermon a second thought. Such a shared reception of Scripture bonds listener and preacher together in a passion for the truth as found in the Bible.

5. Cultivate a Berean attitude. When Paul preached at Berea, "They received the message with great eagerness and *examined the Scriptures every day to see if what Paul said was true*" (Acts 17:11, italics added). Such resolute study makes the Bible come to life, so that each reading offers additional insights for life. Such reading need not be the critical analysis of a prosecuting attorney as much as a receptive reading by a single-minded disciple with a mood of openness that asks, "What does God want me to hear from this passage?"

The Berean plan can be personalized by writing your discoveries in a letter to God. The main divisions of such a letter might include: (1) Thank you, Lord, for what I learned from this passage; (2) help me correct my life according to this Scripture; and (3) I confess the shortcomings I learned from this passage. These letters can be kept in a journal to provide a satisfying record of spiritual progress resulting from encounters with the Bible. Over several weeks, as you mesh the details of your life with the teachings of Scripture, your spiritual development will astound you.

6. Try the Six Questions exercise. This method builds on the journalist's five W's and one H formula, which Rudyard Kipling summarized in *Just-So-Stories:*

> I keep six honest serving men
> (They taught me all I knew);
> Their names are What and Why and When
> And How and Where and Who.

Question biblical passages with who, what, when, where, why, and how. The answers will transform your inner world and deepen the meaning of Scripture for you.

7. Paraphrase a passage. This exercise helps you learn more about life from Scripture because it requires you to carefully consider the meaning of every word in the passage. Chaplain Carl F. Burke, who served for years in a boys' correctional institution near Buffalo, New York, used this technique to make Scripture relevant to delinquent boys from urban slums. Think how one eleven-year-old was affected by his own paraphrase of a portion of Psalm 23: "The Lord is my probation officer. He will help me. He tries to help me make it every day. He makes me play it cool."[7]

Ask yourself as you read, What does the passage say to me? To be most effective, this approach requires that paraphrases be written—writing encourages organization and precision of thought. Some people keep a journal where they record paraphrases and jot down new thoughts for future reading. To write your paraphrase now and read it later deepens its impact and makes you deal with the passage at least twice. In reality, two or more thoughtful encounters with a passage make it reverberate in the inner world for a long time. This practice will likely lead to the joyous discovery that obedience to Scripture is more than a duty; it is also a gloriously satisfying adventure.

8. Make friends of Bible personalities. Every reader remembers an especially influential biographical article or book about a famous person like Washington, Lincoln, Churchill, Truman, or Kennedy that shaped their views of democracy and patriotism. Likewise, Bible personalities like Elijah, Joseph, Paul, and Peter help us know God better and mold our thoughts about forgiveness, hope, and faith.

We can study the strengths, sins, crises, or spiritual influences of Bible characters. The enormous enablement these individuals received from God may be the exact encouragement you need to see you through your current perplexities. How reassuring to learn that at least one Bible character lived through circumstances just like yours.

9. Use your knowledge of Scripture. Like all skills, learning about Scripture expands as it is used. That is why Scripture is easier to retain when it is recited frequently; hearing a sermon becomes more meaningful when it is practiced in life; and discussing the Bible increases one's understanding of its message.

Those who communicate the Bible in teaching, preaching, and witnessing need to internalize its message before they share it. Some serious disciples consider their understanding and use of the Bible as an ascending seven-step ladder: (1) hear, (2) read, (3) study, (4) memorize, (5) reflect, (6) apply, and (7) share.[8]

10. Compare translations. The purpose of translations is to deliver the Bible's message to ordinary people in words they understand. For many, the stately, familiar King James Version, first published in 1611, still remains the best-known, much-loved, and often-used version. For years to come it will doubtless remain their first choice. But new translations open the meaning of Scripture to this generation and communicate its wisdom in words used in everyday life. Modern translations update words that may have changed over nearly four centuries and take advantage of newly discovered older manuscripts that were written nearer the date of the original writings. These are the reasons why new translations may explain the original writer's message more accurately.

Try using various translations to help you trace themes like love, faith, or hope throughout the entire Bible; a concordance or study Bible will help you locate the references. The Bible's comprehensive message on these big themes will prove helpful in your quest to grow a great soul.

As you compare individual passages in various translations, make a commitment to be as thorough as possible in your study of Scripture. John Wesley once received a letter informing him, "The Lord has told me to tell you that He doesn't need your book-learning, your Greek, and your Hebrew." Wesley replied, "Thank you, Sir. I already knew the Lord had no need for my 'book-learning,' as you put it. However—although the Lord has not directed me to say so—on my own responsibility I would say to you that the Lord does not need your ignorance, either."[9]

Serious study of Scripture can be splendid and thorough at the same time. There need be no contradiction between tenderheartedness and tough thought; God welcomes both as sojourners seek to faithfully follow the Manufacturer's Manual. Your life will be more useful and joyful as you follow God's instruction in Scripture. The Bible, much more than a mere book, is a way of life, an encounter with God, a loving correspondence of the Father's plans for His child, and a revelation of what really matters. The Bible is an invitation to fulfillment and a promise of enablement for the authentically good life.

Exercises to Get Your Soul in Shape

- Personalize a passage.
- Enter Scripture as an active participant.
- Develop a personal Bible study method.
- Participate seriously in biblical preaching.
- Cultivate a Berean attitude.
- Try the Six Questions exercise.
- Paraphrase a passage.
- Make friends of Bible personalities.
- Use your knowledge of Scripture.
- Compare translations.

**Put your life
on the line
for your friends.**
John 15:13
(TM)

ഔ

Architect of Affirming Relationships

Thanks for those magnificent individuals who
pointed me to Christ when I questioned
Christianity.
loved me when I went to the far country.
nurtured me when I was spiritually illiterate.
worship in church each week with me.

(Complete this prayer for yourself.)

Open my inner eyes so I may
see what You want in my family concerning . . .
understand what You want in our church
about . . .
commit to what You want in my world of work,
including . . .
Thanks for all the positive influences in my life
from so many people who love You. Amen.

Cherish Relationships

Cultivate Soul Friends

> One of the most wonderful gifts we receive from a soul friend is that of a new perspective. He or she is able to stir up our imagination so that we not only view the past differently, but also allow the future to be filled with new, exciting possibilities.
>
> —*Alan Jones*

Once, when my seminary friend Ford Miller was serving as a student minister at Asbury United Methodist Church in Prairie Village, Kansas, a charming six-year-old girl answered his knock at the door of her home. After helping her mother welcome the pastor, the child called her friends into the house and tried this faltering introduction: "Pastor Miller, these are my friends. I use them every day."

Her social error sounds amusing at first, but, when we think about it, we all use friends every day because we need them so badly. Growing out of an unquenchable hunger for relationships, our actions agree with the admonition found in a "Graffiti" cartoon: "Make good friends before you need them." Friends, as much a part of the human legacy as our genetic makeup, provide a link with what really matters in life and help in our own eager attempts to grow a great soul.

God puts friends and family in our lives to satisfy our inborn need for closeness. He created this capacity in us so that we might cherish each other, and He sometimes helps us see old friends in wonderful new ways. Virginia Coleman expressed affection for her church friends during a prayer meeting this way: "I thank God for you. I never want to get you out of my heart." Even though most of us feel this way deep down, we are often too preoccupied to give adequate attention to the reservoir of relationships that could easily be cultivated into gratifying friendships.

The need for friends is pressingly obvious; well-nourished relationships add to our wholeness and have much to do with keeping us emotionally whole and spiritually well. During a visit to the many gift shops where my wife takes me, I found this wisdom on an unsigned craft plaque: "A friend is one who knows you as you are, understands where you've been, accepts what you have become, and still gently invites you to grow." Such tender ties help blunt the harm modern life does to all of us.

Though friendships come in varying intensities, every relationship, even a passing one, has amazing potential to point us to God. The incalculable benefits—all components of wholeness—include intangible payoffs like affection, trust, respect, mutual aid, understanding, devotion, acceptance, spontaneity, and self-disclosure.

A Latin poet underscores the incredible necessity of tearing down our self-constructed barriers so that others can come in:

I look for God
and I cannot find God.
I look for myself
and I cannot find myself
But I find a friend;
And the three of us
We go on our way together.

Relationships—Remedy for Loneliness

Loneliness, a first cousin to stress, is so common in contemporary life that social science professionals estimate that one hundred million Americans suffer from some degree of social isolation. From experience, most people understand why a nightclub comedian generates laughter when he jokes, "Remember, we are all in this alone." And in the same city, a pop singer sadly admitted in a newspaper interview, "I stand across the stage lights from hundreds of people when I perform, but after the shows I go to an empty room as a prisoner of my success." To feel totally alone is among the worst despairs anyone can experience.

Surprisingly, even those who spend their time in crowds live close to loneliness. Albert Schweitzer, the humanitarian missionary to Africa, once said we are all so much together, but we are all dying of loneliness. Though the concept sounds unbelievable, research says most people have ten or fewer real friends throughout their lifetime; other informal surveys say it may not be more than five. Apparently, lots of people live with an unmet hunger to be close to others whose acceptance does not depend on what they do or say or think—a safe place where they can be themselves.

Yesterday I met a man who appeared to have it all—a fine job, a flashy car, and an impressive address. But he has not seen his extended family and lifelong friends for five years because they are located back home, more than twenty-five-hundred miles away. This space and time distance cause him unbearable loneliness, which he loathes. This man, however, is not alone in his loneliness; he fits the pattern of thousands who are isolated by circumstances beyond their control. One of the most pressing dilemmas of our time is how to establish and sustain the enabling and lasting relationships we all need.

The problem of loneliness is further complicated by the fact that meaningful relationships keep slipping away. Death separates mates and friends. Betrayal breaks relationships. Divorce fractures families. Transitions, geography, or growing apart create an ebb in the intensity of friendships. But as Vernon Grounds explains, "We were not made to live as a recluse, a hermit, or a lone wolf, but in fellowship with our neighbor. We were made to enter into a relationship of love and trust and service with other people. And unless we do this we become emotionally sick, miserable, and frustrated."[1]

Since satisfying associations require constant tending, this loneliness question forces seekers after meaning to rethink ways to nourish friendships. The Bible records the loneliness of stalwart people in many difficult situations: Daniel in the lions' den; Elijah under a juniper tree; John the Baptist in the desert; Paul in a Roman jail; and Jesus in the wilderness in Gethsemane and on the middle cross. These examples make us realize that God fully understands our feelings of isolated detachment, and stands ready with many effective remedies to heal our separation from others.

However, just when loneliness feels like an inner holocaust, God reminds us, "This is ridiculous. You can change this frustration." The remedy is close by in our hearts. Everyone can give the gift of friendship to another individual so that both parties can be healed. Every human being was created with a need to love, touch, and be close to others, and human beings can give these qualities to each other.

Naturally, our efforts to build happy associations sometimes travel over a bumpy, two-way road. The cartoon caption has some truth in it: "A circle of friends usually includes triangles and squares." It is true that healthy relationships start with the tough task of accepting people as they are, but the possibility of finding close friendships is worth paying that price. Beginning at any moment you choose, life can be enriched by making a conscious effort to treat everyone you meet as a potential friend.

Relationships—A Faith Development Laboratory

God created relationships as a testing ground to verify His teachings about family, friends, and church. Relationships, much more than a convenient way to organize society, provide a unique laboratory for developing and using spirituality so that even when human linkages tax our patience, they help us become authentic people, build inner integrity, and strengthen faith. Consequently, every bridge-building effort to develop friendship offers possibilities to improve life with love given and received and often helps us see our relationship with God better.

A Persian proverb offers interesting insights for developing relationships: "We come into the world crying while all those about us are smiling. May we live so that we go out of this world smiling while everybody around us is weeping."

Just as a scientific laboratory proves theories, relationships help us validate ideas about spiritual development and cause us to recognize the unspeakable beauty of each person. John Mogabgab writes, "A friend whose parish is located in Detroit's inner city once observed that when you open your heart to God, you never know who the Lord will bring along."[2] He is right. In this faith development lab among friends, forgiveness becomes as real as light, love proves to be stronger than hate, and hope overcomes doubt.

Far from being a computerized, robotized relational factory, these friendship laboratories demonstrate how difficult it can be to live in harmony with others without divine strengthening. Consequently, the Father sends people to be two-way channels to both give and receive grace, mercy, and affirmation. Such testing teaches us a lot about God, ourselves, and others even as it forces us to consider the counsel of the sixteenth-century Carmelite reformer, John of the Cross: "God has so ordained things that we grow in faith only through the frail instrumentality of one another."

There is also a surprising mutual benefit that grows out of well-lived relationships. Albert Schweitzer explains the astonishing benefits: "Not one of us knows what effect his life produces, and what he gives to others; that is hidden from us and must remain so, though we are often allowed to see some little fraction of it, so that we may not lose courage."[3] Life lived in meaningful association with others offers us a wellspring of satisfaction, while living in isolation makes us wither and die.

Friends, as special gifts from God, sustain us in dark hours, help us cross-examine our thoughts, and lend their support when we are afraid to believe in ourselves or God. Interestingly, others receive the same from us, so lavish benefits flow both ways. Fulfilling relationships provide fertile soil for growing robust faith.

Friends—People Who Point Us to God

Devotional writers, preachers, theologians, and pastors all help us apply spiritual development basics like

Scripture reading, prayer, obedience, loving, fasting, and generosity to the details of life. Bob Benson, however, wants us to add another viable and largely untapped source: "St. Ignatius Loyola taught his followers to seek and find God in all things. But with apology to the Saint, why not seek and find God in every *one*."[4] Other people—anywhere, anytime—offer new ways of seeing God and life. Often God's voice is heard most clearly through close-by human beings who are unforgettable exhibits of love, grace, and forgiveness. Consequently, we must cherish the amazing fact that everyone we meet has a potentially fresh insight from the Father for us.

Friends nourish faith. The endless possibilities come from many unexpected sources. Noble deeds performed by hurting human beings stretch us. Courageous achievements by handicapped people deepen our gratitude to the Father. Gestures of generosity by the poor challenge our use of money. Others' acceptance of us strengthens our belief in ourselves. Surprisingly, we are sometimes impacted in never-to-be forgotten ways by a greeting from a stranger at a supermarket checkout counter, a casual remark by a neighbor, or a thoughtful word from an old acquaintance.

That is why so many ordinary people have such extraordinary influence on our spiritual quest. Once a friend made me understand ethical pressures in modern business practices when he expressed his frustration as we left a politically charged zoning hearing for a new church site: "Pastor, before we get this church built, this political system may make a cheat out of you." Naturally, I questioned his statement, but God reminded me through my friend that snow-white ethics are difficult to maintain in many secular business and political environments.

A little boy deepened my awareness of creation as he looked up from the Broadmoor Hotel pond near Colorado Springs to ask, "Mister, did you ever pet a duck like this?"

The Father taught me through that freckled-faced pre-schooler to marvel and cherish the creation around me.

A year or two after my lifelong friend's wife died at forty-seven, he helped me develop a new appreciation for long-term marriage. I felt the depth of his loss when he said, "Dating at fifty is like taking on a second full-time job." Through my friend, God reminded me to cherish my own marriage more and to celebrate the stable marriages of old friends.

When we listen carefully, our fellow human beings often become a challenging source of spiritual illumination whose words may ring in our hearts for months and years, perhaps even for a lifetime. The most enlightening messages often come from those who have no intention of influencing us. The great pastor, Halford Luccock, is right: "You find yourself in the exciting adventures of the mind opened to you by fine minds who awakened your mind, the riches of friendship given you by those who have walked with you, the sense of responsibility which has grown out of great tasks someone gave you to do, and lift of ideas given you by someone who held them high before you."[5] God uses others to touch us with inspiration and insight, so we become a living mosaic of everyone we have known.

God frequently uses people as mirrors to reflect how we look to Him and others. Psychiatrist Carl Jung once explained "we meet ourselves time and again in a thousand disguises of life." Oswald Chambers, the devotional writer, jars us wide awake when he says, "Our heavenly Father has an amazing sense of humor. He will bring across your path the kind of people who show you what you have been to Him."[6] To accurately receive such data requires an intentional willingness to understand what God is saying through others.

Nearly every relationship stretches our spiritual development in some way. Some associations require strength that we would never develop without the demanding expectations of others. As the child trusts the parent, the adult is forced to grow because he feels unworthy of such trust. When a patient places wholehearted confidence in the physician, the conscientious doctor wonders how to measure up. When a dying saint puts full faith in the minister's words of hope, the pastor feels obligated to move beyond his own inner dryness. And students sometimes stand on tiptoe to be all they can be when their teacher expects them to do well. A friend of mine knew a little fellow who was disruptive and did so poorly in second grade that he was assigned to a new teacher. After a few weeks, his mother questioned his amazing improvement. The boy explained, "My teacher thought I was good, so I was." The hymn writer Howard Arnold Walter had the same idea when he sang, "I would be true, for there are those who trust me."

The Master Potter uses soul friends to develop Christ-likeness in us. This kind of friend is more than an accommodating neighbor who cares for my mail when I leave town. A soul friend is more than an acquaintance who knew me before I started school, met me as a mixed-up college student, or lived down the street in Carmichael, California. Soul friends are much different than my childhood playmates on French Road near Detroit's city airport, parents of my children's friends in Moses Lake, or fellow graduate students at Vanderbilt University.

Soul friends are those with whom I maintain a relationship of such depth that it is quickly revived with only a few sentences even after we have been apart for months or years. Such a bond started with a special "aha" moment in the past when they made a never-to-be forgotten impact on me. From some small beginning, a trust grew between us so that they accept me just as I am, even though they may not fully understand me. These friends provide insights and courage to help me find deeper significance in my journey of faith; they are Christian through and through. This relationship is not better than family ties—just different.

Let me introduce several soul friends who have helped connect the fragments of living into a meaningful whole for me. AFH, old enough to be my father, but once my editor-in-chief, always encouraged me to write; but he made an enduring investment in our friendship when he walked with me to a tiny new grave near Kansas City where we buried my first son, who died shortly before birth. AJW, VH, MH—three women with hotlines to heaven—have taken my desperate needs to the Father's throne and returned with incredible life-changing answers. ESM, gentle spirit and decent human being, my superior and colleague in an important Christian assignment, trusted me so implicitly that I became the person he thought I was. BMS, my absolutely loyal friend for twenty-five years, is embarrassingly extravagant with confidence and affirmation. BB, now with the Father, believed in my Kingdom dreams based on an idealism that probably should have corroded long ago. MAL, my publishing friend for thirty years, helped me build several creative ideas into realities that impacted hundreds of ministers and brought enormous satisfaction. KD, a woman of startling creativity and devotion, first came into my life as a pastor to my college-age sons and now shares a wonderful friendship with their parents. MJK, childhood buddy, adult friend, and faithful nurturer, packed two lifetimes as a soul friend into her less than fifty years.

My list of soul friends is much too long to continue, but I am better because of them—nobler, and more like Christ. With apology to the writer of Hebrews, what more can I say? The world and I are not worthy of them. To be spiritually whole, everyone needs soul friends like mine—persons with whom you can stretch, agonize, and grow. They are available all around us if we are willing to nurture them.

There is another serendipity when someone cares how we live. Helen Hayes understood this give-and-take: "We relish news of our heroes, forgetting that we are extraordinary to somebody, too."[7] Just to be aware that someone knows us and prays for us empowers us to remember and live by what is significant and true. So husbands need wives to appreciate them as much as wives need their husbands' unconditional love. Employees grow when superiors expect greatness, but employers need subordinates to depend on them too. Churches need loving pastors, but ministers are most fulfilled when they serve affirming congregations. Healthy relationships always produce a stimulating two-way street; so real friends help each other grow.

Though every bud of friendship will not ripen into mature fruit, why not welcome every green shoot and enjoy every colorful blossom. The secret is to give and receive as much as possible from every relationship. Accept folks as they are and allow them to determine the depth of their friendship with you. Be grateful for those who share a passing "good morning" on the street corner, cherish those who believe in your cause, and treasure tried-and-true friends of the years. Pay careful attention to each new friendship simply because long-term relationships always begin as casual acquaintances.

The deepest lessons of Christianity are never learned in isolation. It is nearby neighbors, loyal friends, and even casual associates who create warm, affirming climates where spirituality thrives. Think of the possibilities. It happens when teenagers ask, Who am I? and Where am I going? In middle years, relationships provide reassuring support for midlife crises. And when old age approaches, faithful friendships affirm the meaning of life. Though human existence without friends feels like a dreary desert, fulfilling relationships add strength, vigor, and wisdom to life.

Family—A Powerful Place to Grow

Many contemporary families seem to be at war with God's plans for them. Divorce has so drastically changed society that traditional families like the TV Waltons are apparently gone forever. And because 50 percent of mothers of children under eighteen now work outside their homes, their offspring often have more of what they want and less of what they need.

Family alienation has deepened due to vanishing moral and social values; illegitimacy, desertion, promiscuity, divorce, and juvenile crime make the situation frighteningly alarming.

Awareness of old problems like violence, abuse, drugs, and codependency that make families dysfunctional has increased. This tidal wave of family disintegration creates despair for individuals and incredible problems for society. Recently a grown man told me with a wistful sigh that multiple divorces made his family tree look as if it had been hit by lightning. This increasing sense of loss frustrates every level of society even as a new generation grows up at risk.

Restoration of brokenness. Not to oversimplify or unduly complicate the issues, the major problem appears to be brokenness. It is the brokenness rooted in emotional abuse that limits a child's learning and keeps the parents from finding fulfillment in their marriage and family. It is the brokenhearted four-year-old boy in divorce court forced to tell his father good-bye until a visit can be arranged at the whim of his alienated parents. These fractured relationships emphasize the fact that few things are worse than a house that is no longer a home.

In light of such devastation, is it time to seriously reconsider the biblical solution of forgiveness and reconciliation? Could it be that our situation is desperate enough that we are ready to move toward family solidarity and away from selfishness, which satisfies no one? Can we intentionally rebuild loving harmony into our families and churches? Since the drumbeat of broken commitments and societal secularization has brought us to this brink of despair, is it now possible to follow God's call back to sanity, survival, and even satisfaction?

Using spiritual disciplines. Though centuries old, the remedies offered by spirituality hold miraculous cures for this destructive epidemic in our society and in ourselves. Like fine china, a family is beautiful to experience, but easy to mar or break. To paraphrase the Peace Corps slogan, building a family may be the toughest job you will ever love. When seriously applied to life, spiritual resources can help married couples discover that renewed affection between them can be a hundred times better than some fleeting promise of a new love. Parents can discover again that children can be enjoyed rather than endured. Family connections are worth constant nurturing because they affect everything else today, even as they cast a long influence across future generations.

Biological bloodlines do not automatically create a feeling of belonging or a sense of family or lifelong family happiness. Instead, a real family—biological or adoptive—demands hard work that nourishes caring interactions to stimulate the mind, comfort the soul, and shelter the body.

The adventures of parenting. Though parents hold a child's hand for only a few years, the imprint they make on the child's heart lasts forever. And though children may live in the home for only eighteen or twenty years, their effect on parents is eternal. As Peter DeVries put it, "The value of marriage is not that adults produce children, but that children produce adults."[8] This two-way influence between parents and children is more incredible than any family trait carried in genes or chromosomes.

Think of the adventure. Kathy Coffey's essay "With Baby and Briefcase" describes a co-worker's question, "How can you work all day, then go home to your kids?" Though the questioner expected a discouraging litany, she answered, "I couldn't work without them." Then she tells how benefits outweigh exhaustion when her kids shout, "Mom, you look beautiful today," or wait by the walk to show her the first yellow crocuses of spring.[9] Parenting pays special rewards and satisfaction even though it is tough, tiring, hard work.

Having children gives us the perfect excuse to enjoy the special feeling of being a child again—to laugh, to cry, to grow, to learn, and to depend. Maybe God looks on the whole human race and says, "I love children. I want to help children. It doesn't matter if they are eight, twenty-eight, or eighty-eight. They are not brittle, and they take risks." There is something spiritually stimulating about cultivating in ourselves childlike trust, curiosity, and affection toward the Father and the family of God.

The growth possibilities in families. Relationships between children in a family also offer potential for emotional strength and growing a great soul. Brothers and sisters must work to be friends. This need is graphically explained in a letter printed in an Ann Landers' column from Lucille of St. Louis to her sons: "Nobody else will remember the Christmases you had, the tree house you built, the day you learned to ride a bike, the fun you had trick or treating, the teacher you loved in the third grade and the kittens born in the laundry room. There will be only the two of you and you had better love each other now, because sixty years from now only you will remember all the wonderful experiences you shared and those memories will be golden."[10] Such a common heritage of shared experiences provides the foundation for siblings to become best friends. Everyone needs someone like a brother or sister to increase self-acceptance, heal harmful memories, and build abiding values into the fabric of life.

Extended families provide for companionship across generations, too. The elders can have a part in shaping new generations with the family roots they represent; even as the young, with their adventuresome risks, teach the elderly. Regardless of experience or age, persons learn a lot about inner wellness from two or more generations in their families. These possibilities continue throughout the entire life span because today's children will likely become someone's parents, while these same people are forever tied to their parents and grandparents. Such relationships across generations should be nourished simply because everyone stands to receive so much benefit from them.

One grandfather, an influential churchman respected by thousands, remarked shortly after retirement, "Only one's family makes much difference when evening shadows start to fall." How sad, then, that so many approach mature years with little investment in happy family associations. A lonely career woman has sad firsthand knowledge of this problem because she spent inadequate effort in building relationships with her grown children. As a result, in her early sixties she said, "Now I know life is measured by family and not by finance." She suffered lonely alienation during old age because her discovery came too late to start over again. Yet some people wear emotional blinders that keep them from seeing this issue.

A father in his fifties whose sons, since high school, did not suit him with their appearance, lifestyles, or career choices, reasoned, "I'm ready to bury the hatchet.

Whatever their rejection of my standards, they are my sons, and I want to be close for whatever time we have left." An adult friendship started the day he made that decision; his sons entered freely into the new relationship, accepting their father on a more equal basis with shared respect.

A grandmother, forced into second-generation parenting because of her daughter-in-law's death from a pulmonary embolism, shrugs off the acclaim she received by saying, "All I get is a lot of pleasure out of every happiness the grandchildren have." How fortunate for all of them that grandchildren, grown son, and grandmother made life an adventure for each other.

Families keep changing. In family life, because of constant change, there is always more building of relationships to be done. As childhood, parenthood, and grandparenthood fly by, life forces us to let go of some relationships so that we can take hold of others. Each adjustment has its rewards, even though another demand waits around the next corner. Think of the joyous possibilities: I am a better person because these changing circumstances required me to be a grown son, husband, son-in-law, father-in-law, and now grandfather.

Love, acceptance, and commitment in families are as much needed for inner health as food is required for physical health. Author Walter Tubbs is right: "We are fully ourselves only in relation to each other." Though everybody needs something like a family, many moderns exist for a lifetime without experiencing the positive influences a real family offers. Consequently, even though earlier forms of family may be gone forever, rediscovery of the strengths they provide is needed now more than ever.

Everyone needs something like a family to nourish the spirit as much as he or she needs shelter against the sun, rain, and snow. Family trees grow and bear fruit as they are rooted in affection, affirmation, and faith formation.

Church—A Family Everyone Needs

A divorcée in her early thirties moved to a strange city with her young children. Though she longed to begin a new life, her past drove her to places where she formed dead-end relationships. One evening in a near-drunken state, her heart questioned her about the purpose of her existence. At nearly the same moment, a young neighbor couple appeared at her door to offer a cordial invitation to attend church with them the next morning, Sunday. Though she hesitated, their friendly persuasion was hard to resist.

True to the couple's promise, they came the next morning to take the mother and her little family to a small church not too far from her house. As the tiny congregation offered her friendship, she felt drawn to Christ and surrendered the shreds of her broken life to the Savior. Along with her newfound faith, her sense of belonging increased as the people of God offered her unconditional love and overlooked her strange ways. Her new church friends provided such wholehearted support that she began calling them "the family I never had."

Alternative to family breakdown. Such magnetism can be offered by every church as an attractive alternative to family disintegration. In its finest hour, the church authentically becomes the family of God. Then, whenever this family of faith gathers anywhere around the globe, weary wanderers can find a home and join a company of prodigals at the Father's table to enjoy a thanksgiving feast together. With poetic insight, songwriter Bryan Jeffrey Leech rivets these possibilities for reconciliation into our hearts:

> We are God's people, the chosen of the Lord,
> Born of His Spirit, established by His Word;
> Our cornerstone is Christ alone,

And strong in Him we stand.
O let us live transparently,
And walk heart to heart and hand in hand.

Church—a rich relationship. A friendly word like *church*, backed by of two thousand years of tradition, though frequently blundering and sometimes bordering on the barbaric, creates many mental images in conversation, print, or sermon. For some, the word conjures up an arid meetinghouse where institutional preservation reigns supreme. For some, it may trigger memories of joyous weddings or sad funerals. For others, the mere mention of the word *church* produces mental pictures of edifices as diverse as the Cathedral of Notre Dame or the "little brown church in the wildwood." Some people automatically translate the word in their minds to mean Pastor Brown's church. For others, church means a literal sanctuary—a safe space for withdrawal from life. For a frightened few, it may be the last stronghold against change.

Church—spiritual discovery. In its fullest meaning, however, the church is a joyous rendezvous of pilgrims on a journey of spiritual discovery. It is built on the frank admission that going it alone usually means going nowhere in spiritual development, but going together leads to the Giver of harmony who heals destructive memories and painful pasts. Like a glorious family reunion, this going together encourages us to become all we can be.

These meaningful associations resource the authentic church so that it channels the efforts of ordinary people into life-changing exploits. Its worship and proclamation refresh the God-seeker's soul with an expanding vision of Christlikeness. Close ties to the people of God produce hope and provide a sense of personal worth. The most important of all tests for the church is the difference it makes in the daily lives of its members.

Many people are searching for a place to belong because fast-lane living never satisfies in an ultimate sense. Consequently, a real church can never allow itself to become a Peyton Place of gossip or a platform for destructive behavior. A quarreling, bitter church cannot speak to the world about anything. Rather, the church must foster a relational richness in which all kinds of people gather to cherish each other, to discover meaning for life, and to seek God's will. That is what every church can be, a center of acceptance and love.

A family of friends. The church as a family of friends has the dual task of introducing people to divine resources and sensitizing them to human need. In many ways, it Christianizes believers at the same time it offers to remedy the hollow emptiness of spiritually needy people. In stimulating authentic relationships, the church teaches that everything a human being possesses is a gift-loan from God to be used for an individual's good and to be available to others—a powerful prevention against greed. In this extended family, where fellow believers are closer than blood brothers and sisters, being cherished supplies a health-giving antidote for isolation, loneliness, and tension.

Such a Christ-centered family, called the church, offers the instruction of an exciting school where learning is a joy, the healing of a supernatural hospital where inner health is assured, the resources of a wealthy bank where human needs are abundantly supplied, and the acceptance of a home where love is supreme. As a network of happy friends, the church becomes a channel through which people strengthen each other in uniquely satisfying ways.

A community of becomers. The church, by definition and essence, possesses latent power to be a restoring community of "becomers". Vernon Grounds clarifies the issue: "On a human level, every New Testament church is to be family, a fraternity, and a fellowship, whose members share profoundly and pervasively."[11] This means that many facets of the inner world, such as beliefs, aspirations, motives, emotions, and choices, are impacted by this radical association of love in which persons struggle to be godly together. Consequently, these significant relationships test questionable practices and create a climate in which everyone feels valued as a child of God. Inasmuch as this unique blending of divine and human resources cannot be found in other organizations, the church must be encouraged to become what it was intended to be.

Sadly, the church, planned by God to be a resource for spiritual growth, often spends too much energy perpetuating itself. As a result, the stirring adventures of life together are numbed by secondary concerns like larger facilities, expanded programs, or fading traditions. In other equally frustrating situations, the church is sometimes reduced "to either a pep rally for Jesus or an irritating set of restrictions."[12] But an almost irresistible attraction emanates from an authentic New Testament church that is committed to caring for people in place of institutional maintenance. And every church's vigor and health increase as it gives itself to these lofty purposes.

A Christ-centered family. To be the Christ-centered family everyone needs, the church must resist Madison Avenue hype and induced enthusiasm and focus instead on the higher good of obedient worship of God based on Holy Scripture and a vibrant fellowship with one another. This means that cold orthodoxy, meaningless liturgical or evangelical rituals, slick professionalism, empty traditions, and self-centered ecclesiastical power games must be eliminated.

The aim of our Lord was not for the church to create a small, ingrown religious sect, but to bring new life and adventuresome faith to the whole human race. Therefore, in the church, in place of lesser things, the Scripture must be taught with affectionate authority and true-to-life application. Public services must inspire commitment, worship, and praise. The resources of the gospel must be focused meaningfully on God's answers to the mind-boggling problems of modern people. Stuffy forms must be infused with soul-gripping vitality to provide a safe place for self-disclosure, mutual trust, and an openness to the new things God wants to do in every person. And lay and ministerial leaders must together become willing servants of all.

The church, much more than a mere commercial enterprise, is intended by God to be a family of seekers whose reason for being is to help everyone discover supernatural resources for inner wellness. This dormant capability of the local church must be activated to restore troubled people to purposeful living and to lead them into wholeness. The main problem facing the church, then, is to apply its unique resources to the needs of ordinary people.

Because such resourceful relationships are possible and needed, they must be developed. Then empty churches will fill up again. Then faith living will be fun. Then saints will salt society in factories, governments, corporations, and everywhere else. Confused secularists will experience transformation. The Bible will be respected again as the authority for living. Preachers will be reenergized. Once again sin will be forgiven and forsaken. Brokenness will be healed and peace will reign. Participation in these realities of spirituality will end the famine of faith as congregations, families, and individuals pray and sing together again.

The obvious question is, Where can such a church be found? This query must be seriously considered because it implies that such churches do not exist or that the foregoing ideal is unreachable. The most effective answer starts with a hearty effort to improve the church where you attend. Begin by infusing every relationship in that church with the love of Christ. This process develops rapidly when each person begins to feel how deeply he or she is valued and how fulfilling a Christ-saturated life can be.

A society of love. It is a fact of this life together that receiving love enhances the ability to give love, thereby creating a supportive circle of enabling relationships. In such an environment, it becomes almost automatic for people to return affirmation for affirmation, encouragement for encouragement, and affection for affection. Every believer, regardless of talent or training, is called and resourced by God to build these kinds of associations with other Christians. As we meet together in such a fellowship of faith, we enjoy the privilege of saying warm words and doing helpful deeds to encourage others to a deeper appreciation of the gospel, to stronger commitment of servanthood, and to lasting friendships centered in our common love for Christ.

Why not do your part to transform your church into a loving family of God? The fine art of growing such a spiritual family helps people find joy, conviction, and energy in their relationship to Christ and their commitment to each other. This effort makes real the motto of a Colorado church, "Love grows here."

How to Build Spirituality through Relationships

One of the false fantasies of life, fed by unrealistic expectations, makes us believe that someone will soon begin to love us and start a satisfying friendship with us. But because such a wait may be disappointingly long, why not take the lead by reaching out to someone else?

It may be easier to begin than to wait. The time is now, and here are some suggestions on how to get started.

1. Cherish people as God's spokespersons. See every person you meet as a God-given source of inspiration and information. View people as personal spiritual growth inspirers. Value every human being as an important messenger from God to draw you closer to Him. Listen carefully to what they tell you. Give special attention to the young and the elderly who often have wonderful wisdom to share.

2. Cultivate growth friendships. An unidentified veteran of the way offers this wise counsel: "If you want to know God better, keep company with His best friends." Seek out spiritually stable, well-adjusted people as sources of inner development. We all know and try to serve people who deplete our spiritual and emotional energies—they need us. But for your own spiritual growth, your repertoire of friends must also include spiritual strengtheners who will stimulate your faith and bring accountability into your life. Intentionally build associations with those who will be fair and honest in their evaluation of you and will hold you accountable for your commitments in spiritual growth. Apply this Japanese proverb to your spiritual development: "When the character of a man is not clear to you, look at his friends." Live close to spiritually strong people.

3. Use criticism to evaluate your motives. Though critics are seldom comforting, they are often partially accurate. Their discomforting words often contain useful information you can use for self-evaluation. Mistakenly, many of us reject a critic's opinions before checking our inner world to see if the criticisms contain even a shred of needed correction. There is a better way—when criticism is accepted as partially accurate or partially deserved, it shapes our thinking and molds our character. Abba John, one of the desert fathers, helps when he advises us to give up heavy burdens and take on a light burden: "The heavy burden is judging people, the light burden is accepting the judgments of others."[13] Critics can deepen our spiritual development.

4. Accept people as you find them. Though most people are wonderful, Jesus has had a few unusual friends in every past generation, and He still does. To welcome people into your life does not mean you endorse all their actions, nor does it mean you assume responsibility to change them.

Often valuable new perspectives come from unexpected human sources. A New York City street person may have an insight that an ivory tower scholar needs to hear. A new convert imprisoned on death row has something vital to say to believers who came to Christ in childhood. The old have wisdom to share with the young, even as novice Christians and veteran saints have profound insights for each other. Ted Engstrom offers sound advice: "Would we not live wiser, happier, and more fulfilled lives if we enjoyed each other for what the other person is? Young or old, black or white, rich or poor, adult or child."[14] Such interactions sharpen our own spiritual development and make us more loving.

Why not value everyone's uniqueness? Cherish people simply because God created them with such infinite variety. Allow them to be who they are, and catch a glimpse of what they can become by grace. You need never lose the excitement their uniqueness offers because every person will be different each time you meet. Try to live the advice of the old Shaker manuscript of 1848: "Open the windows and doors and receive whomever is sent."

5. Write a relationship journal. Using any form of writing you wish, list three affirming and three difficult relationships in your present circle of friends and family. Simply write your feelings about your experiences with these six people; then lay each summary aside for several days before you evaluate them. Later, when you read them again, you will be amazed to see how your diary provides insights about your own life. We tend to see in others what we like and dislike in ourselves. Thus these summaries will help you sort out what you see in family and friends, but they will also provide a mirror to help you see yourself. Such accurate self-awareness is the first step in self-mastery.

6. Invest love in your church. Though many present-day churches are infected by a sterile rationalism or overwhelmed by a bleak sense of duty, one person sharing *agape* love can quickly revolutionize a church. From a survey of 8,600 people, the Institute of American Church Growth of Pasadena, California, found that "loving churches attract more people, regardless of their theology, denomination, or location." In the same report, church growth specialist Win Arn added, "Love can be taught—and learned—in churches that seem to have forgotten how."[15] In a loving church fellowship, everyone including visitors, newcomers, members, and leaders—gains acceptance, support, and satisfaction. This miracle of loving relationships takes its pattern and power from Jesus.

7. Renew family commitments. A loving family is among life's richest blessings. Apply that beautiful word *family* to all primary relationships—including spouse, children, parents, grandparents, siblings, cousins, aunts, and uncles. And you can develop support groups in the church or community to serve as a substitute family even if your biological family is nonexistent or broken.

Of all the gifts you give to your family, none is as precious as the gift of yourself. Open a line of emotional credit for every member of your real or adopted family in which you become the co-signer, signifying that you will always be available. Then go out of your way to be helpful, to be affirming, and to listen fully. This practice works wonders for all who are involved, because love grows with expression just as commitment expands with practice. Being a loving spouse and a supportive parent are the most important jobs anyone ever had—and among the most satisfying, too. At the same time every family, whether biological or adopted, is a God-given fortress to protect you from stress and spiritual dryness.

Someone in your family connection needs tenderness right now fully as much as you need to give it. Fascinating starting points could be near-kin, rebellious teenagers, grown children, or aging parents. You can help your own soul by doing a loving deed for someone who needs to know you are thinking of him or her. A phone call, written note, or greeting card is a good way to start. Give your family reason to know your support is dependable and lasting. Speak caring words they understand and appreciate. Try affirming them to greatness and strength. Let them know you admire them as friends and that your commitment goes beyond biological connections. Go beyond the call of duty in giving, loving, and serving.

8. Restore broken relationships. Inasmuch as love and forgiveness always start as intentional acts on someone's part, set your will to nurture relationships at home, at work, and in the world. Even though we may not be able to completely control our feelings, we can strengthen even the most sandpapered relationship with Christ-motivated thoughts and deeds.

Avoid anger and retaliation. Like Lincoln, whose heart had "no room for the memory of a wrong," forgive quickly. Enrich each person you meet with an act of unexpected kindness. Rejoice in another person's good fortune as quickly as you would sympathize with his pain or sorrow. Make affirmation and support a habitual part of your conversations. Remember that a two-minute discussion of someone's faults often destroys a lifelong friendship.

When an unfortunate attitude or unkind action fractures a relationship, take the first step toward reconciliation. Your action builds a bridge on which the other person can walk back into your heart. More people than we imagine would like to right a wrong but don't know how to start or don't have the spiritual energy to try. Why not make the first move?

9. Give a gift of presence. Friends ill in body, battered in spirit, or disappointed by life do not need empty words. What they need most is a gentle presence, a listening ear, and a caring heart. Time and attention are among the most precious gifts anyone can give another person. Remember that a gift of presence usually turns out to be a wonderful adventure because the giver often receives more than he gives. Never cease cherishing people; tell them when your heart feels love and gratitude for them.

10. Tackle relational frontiers. Like Columbus in search of new worlds, think of yourself as an explorer searching for ways to build rich relationships or restore fractured ones. Start with broken people near you as prime candidates for friendships, reconciliation, and rehabilitation. Encourage loving interaction in your church. Count your family, regardless of size or closeness, as a center for spiritual development. Friendships, church fellowship, and family are God's solutions to isolation. Try to turn your own loneliness into opportunities for developing satisfying friendships. View distance and mobility as challenges rather than barriers to maintaining friendships; the phone and mail are useful tools to help you succeed.

Relationships really matter when we reduce life to essential basics. Everyone needs to love and be loved.

People are usually wonderful, sometimes strange, and always interesting.

Exercises to Get Your Soul in Shape

- Cherish people as God's spokespersons.
- Cultivate growth friendships.
- Use criticism to evaluate your motives.
- Accept people as you find them.
- Write a relationship journal.
- Invest love in your church.
- Renew family commitments.
- Restore broken relationships.
- Give a gift of presence.
- Tackle relational frontiers.

**Above all else,
guard your heart,
for it is the
wellspring of life.**

Proverbs 4:23

(NIV)

೮ꝛ

Gracious God

Give me a Christ-saturated heart so I can
    love unconditionally.
    serve with loyal devotion.
    persevere obediently for a lifetime.
    pray continually with joy.

(Complete this prayer for yourself.)

Warm my heart so I can live out the spirit of Jesus
    in the details of my life
    in my work including . . .
    in my home including . . .
    in my leisure including . . .
Keep my heart from the evil one. Amen.

Exercises to Make Your Heart Like His

Healthy Hearts Produce Christ-Focused Lives

> When you admit Jesus into your heart, nothing
> is predictable but everything becomes possible.
> —*Henri J. M. Nouwen*

State law required that I have a physical exam so I stopped on my way to youth camp because I had been drafted at the last minute to serve as counselor for ten-year-old boys. "I can't see your heart," the physician joked as he checked my chest X-ray. When I reported the doctor's comment to my friend, who was traveling to camp with me, he retorted, "That's easy to understand—a black heart like yours is always hard to see on X-rays."

Later, as we drove along, my friend discussed a heart-breaking problem in a family we both knew. Soon after arriving at camp, the director called a staff meeting to deal with the heart of an operational problem. Another volunteer could not come to camp because his mother had suffered a heart attack. That day, like many days, that word *heart* kept following us around as we tried to make sense of life.

The physical heart, as familiar as the beating of our pulse, yet as mysterious as our awareness of God, is an incredible bundle of muscles and nerves located left of the center of the chest behind the rib cage. This cardiac wonder, which is about the size of a fist, pumps millions of gallons of blood through the body across a lifetime. This amazing source of physical life keeps a person alive from the first quickening in a mother's womb until the final breath of earthly existence. For good reason, medical science now believes that stress and frustration and emptiness affect the health of your heart and your risk of developing—or even dying from—cardiac disease.

The *heart*, however, is much more than a pump—it's the center of who you are. Heart, in the spiritual sense, describes more than the sum total of all our physical, emotional, or intellectual components; it embraces all three but involves much more. Heart has to do with the essence of our Christlike humanness, the seat of our emotions, the strength of our will, and the seedbed of our spiritual development.

When rational, emotional, physical, and spiritual dimensions of living are combined, it is easy to see that the word *heart* is always at the center of spiritual development in some way, even as it is always at the core of who we are and what we think and say. Everyone understands how the cardiac muscle with four thousand contractions per minute determines physical vitality for a lifetime. And researchers believe the health of your heart and vascular system are at least partly determined by what is on your mind; in other words, scientists are only now beginning to discover what poets and saints have always known about the effect of the heart on all dimensions of life, and the effect of all experiences of life on the heart.

Though the spiritual side may not be so obvious, a pure heart at the core of character is what makes real meaning, significance, and fulfillment possible. Interestingly, my friend's remark on the way to camp about my black heart underscores the way the cardiac and character dimensions converge and affect each other. And inner vagueness and emptiness are common denominators in psychiatry, cardiology, and spirituality.

In the Bible, the word *heart* refers to the inward place of thinking, loving, and deciding—the inner place where affection, emotion, passion, conscience, and faith meet and grow together. Heart, in biblical vocabulary, refers to the center of moral, spiritual, and intellectual life—the seat of emotions, beliefs, and decisions. Since this word *heart* refers to the hidden depth of life, interior confusion and ambiguity clearly must be more than simply ailments of the physical heart. From beginning to end, the human experience compels us to give extra attention to the scriptural proverb that unites the spiritual and physical dimensions of a satisfying life: "A heart at peace gives life to the body" (Prov. 14:30).

Jesus diagnosed heart ailments when He quoted Isaiah with approval, "These people honor me with their lips, but their hearts are far from me" (Mark 7:6). These words, to His hearers and to us, undercut enslaving attention to external customs, regulations, traditions, rituals, and rules. Those same words also teach the inward reality of spirituality, based on the assumption that a good heart produces satisfying Christian attitudes and authentic actions. All this helps us understand that just as the physical heart is the propelling force of blood to keep the human body healthy, the Christ-centered inner heart is the enabling source for wholeness in the moral, spiritual, and intellectual dimensions of life.

In pointing the way to the truly good life of Christ-centeredness, a seasoned minister preached, "The matter of the heart is the heart of the matter." Amazingly, every difficulty of the heart—physical, emotional, or spiritual—produces some degree of inner illness. Conversely, spirituality always lowers and sometimes eliminates anxious tension. That is why our thinking about the heart must take in all of life if we want to experience the full possibilities of inner wellness. Therefore, a regimen of exercise and prevention to produce a strong spiritual heart includes the intentional application of love, faith, and hope to details of daily existence. The choice is stress or spirituality, despair or trust, anxiety or confidence.

A Heart Transplant—Begin with Conversion

The issue of conversion, God's offer of a revolutionary new beginning, must be faced before spiritual development can be seriously started. Christianity, according to Paul Scherer's wise observation, has "for 2,000 years been hawking its wares: New lives for old! If it cannot make good there, it cannot make good, period! That is what it is about. And it is about nothing else."[1] True spirituality begins with a life-changing encounter with Jesus Christ, a kind of spiritual heart transplant that integrates the inner world and gives meaning to the outer world.

With stunning accuracy, Jesus diagnosed a universal need and prescribed a miraculous cure for Nicodemus, a distinguished religious leader of his time. Using plain words, Christ called His cure a new birth. To this day, a sense of hope excites seekers as they read this candid conversation between Jesus and Nicodemus (John 3:1–21); in this incisive incident they see themselves and

God. Simply but significantly stated, conversion changes human character so radically that new values shape thought and behavior—it is a brand-new way of living and thinking. This transformation impacts human existence and relationships at the deepest level. Far from diminishing life, conversion leads into a deeper relationship with God, and an indescribable awareness of integration and peace comes with it.

Such an encounter with Christ profoundly impacted Leo Tolstoy, the Russian novelist, who explained his faith journey in his book *My Religion*: "Five years ago faith came to me; I believed in the doctrine of Jesus, and my whole life underwent a sudden transformation. What I had once wished for I wished for no longer, and I began to desire what I had never desired before. What had once appeared to me right now became wrong, and the wrong of the past I beheld as right. . . . My life and my desires were completely changed; good and evil interchanged meanings."

Conversion does that for everyone; it revolutionizes commitments and transforms values so that the character traits of Jesus show up in us. Oswald Chambers states his bottom-line conviction, "If Jesus Christ cannot alter a man's disposition, Christianity is a cunningly devised fable."[2] And he is right.

Human beings without Christ as Center are likely to encounter such confusion and meaninglessness that they become unsatisfied secularists, or they start to chase religious fads, new cults, or enticing gurus. Though we find it easy to classify ourselves using religious labels like Catholic, Methodist, Baptist, Lutheran, or charismatic, it is easy to embrace a religious system without a Savior or agree to doctrinal propositions without the Person. E. Stanley Jones, the influential Methodist missionary to India, believed that many "know about God but do not know Him; know about moral laws but are powerless to fulfill them."

Apparently thousands live by the untested assumption that if they are good all their lives, everything will work out. This seductive theory lulls people into mushy, undemanding religious thought or activity that produces absolutely no impact on daily life.

In contrast, true conversion transforms low-grade ambiguity and confusion about nebulous religion into vital faith. It calls people to the adventure of integrating the human journey around Christ, who requires a person to live life His way. Erasmus, an aide to the Reformers of the early sixteenth century, explained, "By a Carpenter mankind was made, and only by that Carpenter can mankind be remade." Such a conversion encounter makes it possible to trade trivial pursuits for a purposeful pilgrimage with the living Christ and opens the clenched fist to accept God's helping hand.

Meaning starts at conversion and dramatically increases as spiritual development follows.

Heart Therapy—Talk to Yourself

People talk to themselves—watch drivers at stoplights or pedestrians as they walk along. Internal conversations, which no one sees or hears, are even more common. These interior discussions have the power to shackle or free us as we analyze situations, question experiences, debate alternatives, reinforce fears, and cultivate dreams. In fact, human beings possess the ability to talk themselves into full-blown despair by using deceptive self-dialogue. On the contrary, Christ-centered self-talk remedies our inner chaos.

Destructive inner monologues make us believe malicious lies or reinforce old, entrenched attitudes. This happens when injurious information, like a worthless antique phonograph record, gets stored in our minds for instant replay at a moment's notice. We replay the old script and for some self-defeating reason we enjoy the lyrics, sing the sad songs and remember the old pain; we even relive the old suffering again and again. Some self-talk recordings keep repeating, "Don't try because you always fail."

Information out of our past tries to convince us that we are too tall, too short, too young, too old, too stupid, too smart, or too something. Then we believe crippling notions like, "You ruined your life by marrying the wrong person," or "You are a bad parent because of your rebellious children." Surprisingly, many of these overused records started with people who have been in the cemetery for decades.

Self-talk proves to be especially seductive for those in positions of authority or leadership. Just because an individual has dominant control as a parent, city official, senator, or religious leader does not mean that person is always right or helpful. Conscientious leaders, therefore, need to ask themselves, "Am I seeking the well-being of those I lead?" Such self-interrogation increases a leader's authenticity and decreases the possibility of self-deception.

For some strange reason, some individuals prefer self-delusion to facts. John W. Gardner put it this way: "More often than not we don't want to know ourselves, don't want to depend on ourselves, don't want to live with ourselves."[3] If his assessment is even partly accurate, honest self-talk is desperately needed to help us cope with modern life.

To make self-talk useful, try eavesdropping on yourself to get rid of destructive inner statements like "I'm dumb, stupid, lazy, or weak." Add ideas like "I am loved" and "I can do it." Allow your self-talk, like a conversation with a trusted friend, to question your exaggerations, explore alternatives, and commend your strengths. Give yourself a pep talk based on your faith and aspirations. Remember, the self-doubting voice within is under your control.

To speak the truth to yourself, check the facts and challenge your preconceived assumptions and stereotypes. Ask yourself, "Am I creating a problem or keeping it going to get sympathy, gain attention, or get even with someone?" Admit vulnerability. Resist self-pity because it generally builds on unreliable data originating from a limited perspective or personal prejudices. Using happy memories, replay good times. Add ideas like challenge and opportunity. Remind yourself that accurate self-talk is a tool for converting confusion into strength.

To practice constructive self-talk, try conversations like these:

"I am God's creation, and He makes no junk."

"I always do my best. Sometimes that is not good enough, but everyone makes mistakes."

"I have a missing Center of spirituality, but I am on a quest to find Him."

"I can control my reactions; I refuse to let other people determine the quality of my day."

"I have problems with the proper use of authority over other folks, but I can improve."

"I am needed by someone."

"I am making a valuable contribution to my family."

Accurate self-talk may lead to confession, which brings forgiveness and generates strength for a new start. A country preacher shared an important strategy for strengthening your heart: "You always get further with God when you tattle on yourself."

Heart Treatment—Accept Duplicity in Others and Avoid It in Yourself

The possibility of duplicity, an essential disharmony between one's inner self and outer self, exists in every relationship. William Blake warns: "A truth that is told with bad intent/Beats all the lies you can invent." It happens with frightening frequency on nearly every level of human experience. Children deceive parents. Parents mislead children. Professionals slant news to get ahead in their jobs. Government officials play cheap politics in place of practicing noble statesmanship. Physicians care more about money than about healing the sick. Sadly, duplicity even exists in many churches.

Confusing double-dealing is not new, however. Even during the earthly ministry of Jesus, religious leaders who professed a high interest in truth tried to trick Him with loaded questions about Jewish customs. Their pretended concern for Sabbath laws had nothing to do with their hidden agenda; their questions were calculated traps intended to undercut His revolutionary impact on their vested interests. Eventually, double speech exposed their crafty schemes and downright wickedness.

The apostle Paul experienced similar difficulties. From jail he acknowledged that some preachers proclaimed Christ out of envy and rivalry, intending to stir up trouble while he was imprisoned. This duplicity, however, had little effect on the apostle, who concluded, "What does it matter? The important thing is that in every way, whether from false motives or true, Christ is preached. And because of this I rejoice" (Phil. 1:18).

Many painful examples of mixed motives can be found in Scripture, church history, and personal experience. Why, then, should we be surprised to find seeds of duplicity in every human contact?

After admitting the existence of duplicity, your own heart can be significantly helped by taking a nonjudgmental attitude toward those who perpetuate it. Jesus insisted that judging another's intentions is God's work alone. Perhaps His reasons take into account the ultimate fairness of God and our inability to understand all the facts.

Three important issues must be remembered about judging: (1) the fact that our assessment may be wrong, (2) the possibility of our own self-deception, and (3) the fact that we are not ultimately responsible for another. Because conduct-shaping factors sometimes trick even the most conscientious among us, Thomas Merton claims, "Every one of us is shadowed by an illusory person; a false self."[4] He is right; who is not at least partially confused when asked, "Why did you do what you did?" or "Why did you say what you said?"

Immeasurable help for dealing with duplicity, both in others and in ourselves, comes as we pray with C. S. Lewis, "May it be the real I who speaks; may it be the real Thou that I speak to."

How, then, can the frustration caused by duplicity be reduced? Begin by cherishing the lofty intentions and generous actions of those you have known. Pattern your life after God's gracious forgiveness, and give up your judgments about other people. Try to forget the imperfections of others. As a result, crippling tensions will decrease because your energy will no longer be invested in assigning blame for duplicity. Inner peace is nourished in our inner world when we leave others and their motives to God without judgment. Wholehearted acceptance of all those we meet comes when we assume that duplicity in other people originates from confused motives rather than intentional deceit.

For ourselves, however, we must keep asking, Are my words something I would say to Jesus? Would He see through my wrongheadedness, my revenge, my self-defense, and my conformity? His forgiveness makes me willing to overlook double dealing in others. But in myself, I must face the fact that Jesus is always what He says He is, and I must work with the premise that the Lord expects the same in me.

Heart Exercise—Refurbish Your Inner World

"Instead of waiting for someone to bring flowers, plant your own garden and decorate your soul" is good advice from an anonymous writer. Hanging on the wall of Mother Teresa's clinic, The Place of the Pure Heart—Home for Dying Destitutes, is a verse written by a Hindu poet:

> If you have two pieces of bread,
> Give one to the poor,
> Sell the other,
> And buy hyacinths
> To feed your soul.

Assuming everyone agrees that the soul needs to be refurbished, how can it be done? Some recommend that assertiveness, dominance, and intimidation should rule our attitudes, thoughts, and relationships. According to this line of reasoning, Christian qualities like self-denial, servanthood, and humility are worthless. Such guidance, however, only frustrates weak people who are told to be strong. They wonder how they can pull themselves up by their bootstraps when they have no boots.

In many ways, spiritual development is like other types of self-help because it requires a great deal of personal effort. But there is one important difference—spirituality supplies sufficiency. That means partnership with God provides enablement at the same time as it encourages an awareness of our importance to God. Then, fear of the future fades with the knowledge that the Helper will be in every tomorrow. Freedom to live the way God planned—with His help—is a thousand times more satisfying than doing our own thing.

God offers many underused disciplines for refurbishing the inner life. At first these resources sound overly simple, so something bigger, newer, and more sophisticated is sought. But Merton explains, "The really new is that which, at every moment, springs freshly into new existence. What is really new is what was there all the time."[5]

Therefore, just as a mature vocabulary uses a simple alphabet, true inner refurbishing starts and continues with the old but ever-new exercises of prayer, Bible reading, and meditation. Anyone can use these resources to refurbish his or her inner world. They are ours for the using; what God provides is all we need.

Heart Healing—Deal with Addictions

Addictions grip contemporary people, and we feel anxious about the way they affect our friends, our family, and us. An addiction is any fixation of mind or body that commands so much importance that normal functioning is not possible and spiritual development is neglected or nonexistent. The list of possible addictions is long. Nearly everyone is hooked on one or more compulsions; it could be too much jogging, reading, working, or housecleaning. Addictions result from destructive habits that need to be corrected by a sense of balance in the ways we spend our time, energy, and money.

The damage caused by alcohol, nicotine, and narcotics is obvious; but what about misused prescriptions and food as the drug of choice? Not-so-obvious addictions range from negative attitudes, to feelings of inadequacy, to being a workaholic. Television addictions range from soap operas, to sports, to religious programming. Athletic events can enslave both participants and spectators. Gossip addiction causes good people to believe unfounded rumors, judge neighbors, and read scandalous newspapers or questionable magazines. Some people are bound by addictions that pass for normal behavior, such as an unquenchable desire for prestige or money. Though these addictions may not visibly chain people, they nevertheless imprison the inner life.

Addictions create barriers to wholeness that tense the body, dull the mind, and shackle the soul. The first commandment calls for renunciation of lesser gods, even those that appear to be insignificant to us; Hebrews urges us to desert "besetting sins" (12:1, KJV); and an Indian proverb instructs individuals to "call on God, but row away from the rocks."

Uncontrolled appetites for food, alcohol, sex, money, power, or anything else ultimately destroy individuals. Though an addiction may taste sweet, it is a deadly poison nonetheless. Therefore, if one is to enjoy a genuinely quality life, both subtle and blatant hindrances must be pruned. Paul's firm resolve must be ours, "I will not be mastered by anything" (1 Cor. 6:12). That is the reason why Susanna Wesley taught her children these lessons from Thomas à Kempis: "Whatever weakens your reason, impairs the tenderness of your conscience, obscures your sense of God, or takes off the relish of spiritual things; in short, whatever increases the strength and authority of your body over your mind—that thing is sin to you, however innocent it may be in itself."[6] The advice is valid in every generation for all ages. One stops by stopping, aided by the resources God provides. Corrupting addictions must be deserted if one wants to have a healthy heart and enjoy a singing soul.

Heart Exercise—Turn Duty to Delight

Nagging reminders of duty lurk in many corners of our minds. The buzzwords—*oughts* and *shoulds*—create inner strife when used by parents, spouses, children, bosses, pastors, or teachers. Strange but true, we even use *ought* and *should* on ourselves. Perhaps the taproot of this imprisonment of the soul starts when children are taught that good manners and saved allowances are absolute necessities for a satisfying life. Or the seeds of this tension may begin when harassed teachers try to civilize a class by scolding those who talk and punishing those who do not finish their work on time. Though the origin makes interesting speculation, the reality of this fixation on duty causes second-class living for lots of folks.

Inasmuch as responsibilities cannot be denied, how can these stifling feelings about duty be avoided? We can start by cultivating a perspective that turns duty into delight, including the duties of marriage, parenting, and vocations.

Though the marriage ideal has been severely shattered in much of contemporary society, it starts and continues by keeping serious vows for a lifetime. Marriage is indeed an obligation, but it is also a wonderful privilege that nourishes our inborn hunger for closeness. This enriching obligation turns to delight when both spouses see marriage as an adventure to help them be fulfilled human beings together.

A child, the fruit of parents' love, imposes demanding long-term responsibilities that begin with a birth cry and last until death separates generations. Potential parenting tensions continue or even increase through preschool nurturing, grade school demands, teenage development, and young adult independence. But so much more is possible. If they look for it, parents can experience continuing joy at every point of the journey. Few things are more satisfying than forging lifelong bonds with one's children.

Jobs offer another opportunity to develop wholesome perspectives about duty. In modern society, time and skills are pledged for paychecks, so the way people view work substantially affects their satisfaction with life.

Some workers dislike their jobs so much that they constantly fret about how life evaporates for them even as they mark time until next Friday, another vacation, or retirement. There must be a better way. Who wants a physician, mechanic, preacher, or pharmacist who views work as dreary drudgery?

Occupations can be expressions of service to fellow human beings and to God. On this point, one spiritual master suggested, "Work occupies the body and mind and is necessary for health of the spirit. Work can help us pray, if we work properly."[7] The difference between delight and drudgery takes place as we infuse meaning into our work. An unexpected inner force energizes those who do their work with joy, so that the promise becomes a reality: "I can do all things through him who gives me strength" (Phil. 4:13).

Every individual is obligated to find ways to change duty to fulfillment and responsibility to meaning. Begin by seeking to build satisfying purpose into your responsibilities; as a consequence, your body will benefit from a slower heart rate, deeper breathing, and relaxed muscles. Other advantages may include a happier family, a satisfied boss, contented customers, and an easygoing relationship with co-workers.

Heart Exercise—Choose Your Reactions

Think how you felt when you had an unexpected meeting with a German shepherd, narrowly missed a car wreck, or heard a knock at your door at 2 A.M. In moments like that, you have three possible reactions as your body goes on automatic stress alert: fight, flight, or adapt. For example, when you meet the dog, you could (1) grab a stick to fight; (2) adapt by using Henry David Thoreau's advice, "When a dog runs at you, whistle for him"; or (3) run fast enough to earn a place in the *Guinness Book of World Records*. Survival might very well depend on choosing the right reaction.

All management of frustration requires some degree of choice. When harassment shows up in the workplace, you can fight to change conditions, resign, or accept a bad situation. A fight for improvement might cause your dismissal or bring about needed changes. Flight may result in a better opportunity, but adaptation might condition you to become apathetic or careless. Every response forces stress-generating chemicals into your physical systems, and every choice causes some internal consequence.

It is clear that the only appropriate response in some stress-producing situations is withdrawal. Sometimes parents find their teens' peer pressure at school so harmful that they relocate. Sometimes, after all attempts at reconciliation fail, relationships deteriorate so that a person has to withdraw. Frequently, in difficult situations, flight choices, such as a change of setting or time off, provide the only answer.

On other occasions the only alternative is to take an uncompromising stand. Many problems of society wait for someone to champion important causes. Good people cannot allow the world to get worse simply because they wish to avoid unpleasantness; the question is when and how to take a stand. The potential results of all stand-and-fight responses must be carefully evaluated because they can have such a far-reaching impact on both the outer and inner worlds.

What you do to other people, what you allow people to do to you, and what you think about circumstances determine what stress does to you. To lower stress, match your expectations to the realities of the environment. Martha Washington once observed, "The greater part of our happiness or misery depends on our disposition and not on our circumstances." And she is right. You may not be able to control all stress-creating situations, but you do control the intensity of your feelings and responses. You can change: shift work loads, rewrite schedules, and when interior problems seem to be building, you may try a temporary dropout. Your reactions determine the consequences.

Heart Exercise—Start a Cheering Section

Since tensions feed a fear of failure, a well-paced cheer by a friend or family increases self-confidence and lowers stress. Though cheering sections are common in athletics all the way from Little League to the majors, the need to receive and give affirmation is grossly neglected in other areas of life. Consequently, an expression of praise possesses impact all out of proportion to the effort required to give it. For most people, praise is too rare and criticism is too common. Everyone needs someone to cheer for them most of the time. A pat on the back increases emotional energy and decreases tension.

Though everyone needs someone to recognize a victory in him, we mistakenly think a compliment will embarrass the praised person, so we either preface affirmations with apologies or withhold them altogether. I once met a person who summarized what most of us are reluctant to admit: "Even if I am embarrassed, I always remember praise because it makes me feel so good."

Think how encouragement torpedoes discouragement and despair: compliments make students study harder, praise helps journalists write better, encouragement inspires instructors to teach more effectively, tender affirmation encourages a pastor to preach better, and applause makes athletes play harder. The biggest bonus of all, however, goes to the affirmer. Everyone needs a cheer, and everyone needs to lead a cheer.

Heart Exercise—Reject Spiritual Competition

Contests hound us from the cradle to the grave in our get-ahead society. Babies are judged by when they walk, talk, or cut their first tooth; some communities even sponsor beauty contests for toddlers. Children are compared in terms of grades, I.Q. scores, and height. Teens are pressured by athletics, appearance, and grades. Women judge each other by clothing, size of house, or behavior of children. And grown men compete with job titles, cars, or racquetball scores.

Comparison causes destructive problems at home, at work, at school, and in the marketplace; even inexpensive bowling and golf trophies negatively impact someone. Deep down, people keep asking, "Why can't I be as good as someone else in sports, art, or love?" Others revise the question, "Why don't I get the breaks when I am as good as those who do?" These comparisons create unnecessary frustrations throughout all the stages of life.

When the passion for competition almost does us in, it is useful to consider the view of journalist Sydney J. Harris: "However diverse their talents, temperaments, and differences, all great achievers have one trait in common: they never bother to compare themselves with others, but are content to run their own race on their own terms." Why not follow his idea by judging your spiritual development only by your own progress and potential?

Because God has no favorites, He has little interest in the comparisons we create for ourselves or others. To underscore the issue, Jesus recounted a story about two men who went to the temple to pray. The Pharisee, well remembered for pompous piety, prayed, "God, I thank you that I am not like other men—robbers, evildoers, adulterers—or even like this tax collector. I fast twice a week and give a tenth of all I get." When his fellow worshiper, a tax collector, prayed, he would not even look to heaven, but he beat his breast and cried, "God have mercy on me, a sinner." After telling this incident, Jesus explained His position on spiritual competition: "I tell you that this man, rather than the other, went home justified before God" (Luke 18:11–14). Descendants of the Pharisee, still regrettably active, continue to sidetrack the personal spiritual formation of many conscientious disciples.

Comparisons, even self-inflicted, stymie spiritual growth for timid souls who believe their piety has to be like the most mature Christian they know. Others who seriously seek to connect practical life with faith are turned off by brash moral pygmies who claim to be spiritual giants by comparing themselves with others. How mistaken all of this is. Real saints never keep score, never contrast others unfavorably to themselves, and never brag of what they do or think. Authentic spiritual development always takes into account the fact that people differ in capacities, gifts, and inner needs. Ralph Waldo Emerson said, "God enters by a private door into every individual." Strugglers after God experience unspeakable peace when they are no longer pressured to be a carbon copy of someone else but seek and find their own strategies for inner life development from God's amazing smorgasbord of spiritual resources.

Realistically, there is no need to mimic admired saints because spiritual formation ripens according to individual distinctives. In fact, spiritual masters like Francis of Assisi, St. John of the Cross, Evelyn Underhill, Rufus Jones, and Thomas Kelly had almost nothing in common

except their determined quest to know God more intimately. Consequently, it is useful to apply George Mac-
Donald's view to our journey of faith: "I would rather be
what God chose to make me than the most glorious crea-
ture that I could think of. For to have been thought
about—born in God's thoughts—and then made by God
is the dearest, grandest, most precious thing in all thinking."[8] This mysterious reality encourages every pilgrim
to actualize his spiritual potential to its fullest at his own
speed.

Stress goes down when comparisons are eliminated
and we seriously sing the prayer, "Oh, to be like Thee!"

Heart Exercise—Join the Towel Company

Servanthood, as it shouts from the pages of Scripture,
is God's crowning pattern for finding fulfillment. Christ's
teaching on the subject rings true to everything we know
about human experience: "The greatest among you will
be your servant" (Matt. 23:11). That means service is a
helpful deed we do for a fellow human being, a gift we
give to God, and a satisfying favor we do for ourselves.

Life is exhilarating when a great cause consumes us.
This idea is captured by the English statesman, James
Bright: "You should link yourself to a great cause; you
may never do the cause very much good, but the cause
will do you a great deal of good." This law of life, tested
by thousands of serious Christian disciples, helps us
understand that serving is a boomerang—the more we
give, the more we receive. To give is to grow, and service
saves us from the embarrassment of having God ask what
we did with the benefits He gave us.

The Towel Company, though its objectives may seem
hopelessly out of date, started in the heart of Jesus. To
become a Towel Company member requires no stock pur-

chases, initiation ceremony, or well-connected recommendations. It simply starts by doing something for someone else in the name of Jesus. The servant of Christ, by such action, rejects a widely accepted notion that one individual cannot affect society. He can. In fact, one social scientist recently expressed the opinion that the quality of a whole culture can be changed when only 2 percent of the population have a new vision of what needs to be done and started doing it. The possibilities are mind-boggling.

In this Towel Company, a long history of people have proven that selfless service is the main characteristic of greatness. By example, our Lord taught that humble service leads to true nobility and self-giving is the only path to fulfillment. This amazingly uncomplicated strategy for changing the world, meeting human need, and developing the individual Christian calls us simply to do whatever needs doing for Jesus' sake.

A possible destructive sidetrack must be avoided, however. Soon after they start, some disciples are duped into believing that position, power, and prestige are desirable ends in themselves. Such worldly lusts, regardless of their high-sounding descriptions, never saved a soul, never brought a drug addict to health, never mended a broken family, never healed a sick child, never helped a troubled teenager through turbulence. Every serious Christian needs to hear Eugene H. Peterson's powerful sentence, "The apostles were sensitive to the needs of ministry but indifferent to matters of publicity."[9] Think of the tragedies. Everyone knows of painful examples where status struggles wrecked churches, frustrated mission enterprises, crippled families, and destroyed dreams. Regrettably, vast energies that could have impacted the world for right were wasted chasing the fool's gold of control and notoriety. Control and notoriety for what? Or for whom?

Jesus offers an intriguing alternative when He asks His serious servants to spend themselves without thought of gain. Francis of Assisi proved that a fascinating life could be built on an amazing secret: "It is in giving that we receive."

A plaque displayed on the wall of a senior citizens' center amplifies the idea: "We wish to be involved, to seek, to quest, to adventure, to serve, to laugh at death. Let it come! We have lived!" The authentic servant of Jesus, regardless of age or experience, knows he becomes rich by giving himself away.

Sarah Patton-Boyle, in a delightful description of putting her shoulder to another's wheel, defends the biblical ideal of the togetherness in service in the body of Christ: "When we fail to contribute to the welfare of another, we separate ourselves from the circulatory system, the nerve impulses, and the energy of the whole. When we opt for non-service, we condemn ourselves to internal isolation."[10] Helping another diminishes personal stress at the same time as it forges bonds of relationship; each personal struggle seems easier when someone stands beside us.

Healing for jumbled emotions and unfocused intentions often starts with a simple decision to resign from the rat race that seeks to control others on the job, in the family, and in the church, and instead to serve others in the name of Jesus. Albert Day gives a formula for facing each fresh day without pressure: "Develop the habit of doing and being everything for His sake; loving people because He loves them; doing your work well because He loves excellence; being patient under provocation because that pleases and honors Him."[11] To the noble goal of being like the Master, members of the Towel Company find joy in giving creative imagination and honest toil.

Cardinal Newman describes the bedrock foundation of the Towel Company: "God has created me to do Him some definite service. He has committed some work to me which He has not committed to another. . . . I am a link in a chain, a bond of connection between persons. He has not created me for naught. I shall do good. I shall do His work."

A newsman, assuming the solution to the problem of stress must be complex, quizzed an eminent psychiatrist about what the physician would do if he felt a personal emotional disorder coming on. The doctor's surprising reply fits the "towel teachings" of Jesus exactly: "I would close my office, go to the wrong side of the tracks, and help someone who is worse off than I am. And I would get well." This same idea appears in another form in the writings of Henri Nouwen who, after discussing the temporary usefulness of crying when trouble comes, says, "The ideal remains not to be concerned with yourself, not to cry, not to express all your emotions, but to forget your own problems, and do the work which calls for your attention and interest."[12] Spirituality always flourishes when the focus of life moves from self to others and to God.

Service in the Towel Company is devotion dressed in work clothes. Much more than another duty for a crowded schedule, servanthood is the God-given satisfaction that comes from doing a task for one of the Father's hurting people. Every effort done for another in Christ's name— an affirming note, a thoughtful deed, a caring phone call, a visit to a shut-in, an act of mercy, an encouraging hug, or a shared insight from Scripture—bonds giver, receiver, and God together. Then satisfaction and strength flow between all three parties. Servanthood transforms our efforts for others into fulfilling personal exhilaration.

Heart Recuperation—Renew Yourself

Well before forty, many give up creative ideas, reject new thoughts, and stop developing spirituality. "Too many times around the track, too few new challenges" is the way John W. Gardner describes it.[13] Then for the remainder of their days, these persons reside in self-made prisons where they wall themselves in by familiar surroundings, dull relationships, and grim boredom. Though they do not experience coronary failure or overexertion, they die by inches as hope disintegrates and dreams crumble. Of them Fulton J. Sheen says, "The fires are going out; our salt is losing its savor."[14] Then, in spite of apathetic appearances, they are anxious and tense. What a waste for those whom God created to soar, to sing, and to adventure.

Deep within, a wistful regret chides this willingness to settle for deadly mediocrity. God challenged these faulty assumptions when He planted renewal in every heart just as surely as He put life into ugly tulip bulbs. Like crocuses push their way through late winter snowdrifts, the Father means for us to be called to arms by an insistent inner force that quizzes every acceptance of the status quo. Personal renewal fueled by spiritual disciplines may be the only weapon strong enough to stand against the dehumanization and secularization so common in this period of history. But it is more than enough.

Renewal, however, must be seen for what it actually is. If viewed as just another duty, renewal will only lengthen the long list of responsibilities that compete for our energy and attention. If that happens, the results will be zero. But if spiritual renewal is understood to offer meaning to life, most people may be ready to try.

The needed renewal requires that faith resources be applied to the inner world to deal with hostile criticism, work overload, encroachments on time, fatigue, invasion of privacy, and defeated dreams. Deadly mediocrity changes into renewal when we pray:

> O Wind of God, come bend us, break us,
> Till humbly we confess our need;

Then in Thy tenderness remake us
Revive, restore, for this we plead.
—*Bessie P. Head*

Getting Your Heart in Shape

Getting and keeping in shape has become a billion-dollar business, a national obsession, and a way of life. To diagnostic, prescriptive, and surgical skills, the medical profession has added nutrition, prevention, and exercise to help us learn how to get fit and keep healthy. Now everyone knows wellness is desirable, possible, and to a large degree dependent on one's life-style. But what resources are available to prevent moral, spiritual, and intellectual heart trouble?

For spiritual development, God promises, "I will give you a new heart and put a new spirit in you" (Ezek. 36:26). Spirituality's powerfully effective prescriptions for interior wellness include prayer, worship, and reading Scripture, all of which enable us to function simply and joyfully in our pressure cooker environments. These remedies work when applied to all kinds of nerve-racking circumstances that are an inevitable part of modern life. These spiritual antibiotics destroy dreaded infections of worry and deadly viruses of poorly constructed priorities that grow so silently in our unhealed wounds and overscheduled commitments. These immunizations prevent soul sickness by providing life-changing alternatives to our preoccupations with pleasure and comfort. And God offers prevention as well as radical corrective surgery. Faith formation cures lots of moral heartbreaks with a wonderful blend of pure intention and divine empowerment.

Prayer and Scripture lessen many germs and viruses that attack our inner and outer worlds. Evelyn Underhill advised, "Remember you hold your body and nervous system in trust from God and you must treat His property well." To another she wrote, "Be one-tenth as kind to yourself as you were to me and you will do nicely." When life is centered in Christ, the heart experiences less wear and tear from secular activity. At the same time, it grows strong with strenuous service. Vital faith strengthens the heart against ravaging breakdowns resulting from hurry and strain. Spirituality provides holistic soundness at its best.

To clarify these issues, a final question must be considered: What is the desired outcome of spiritual development for the individual? Inasmuch as spiritual disciplines are not ends in themselves, their faithful practice is not proof of inner wellness any more than long hours of piano practice is evidence of a great musician. Keeping score or even breaking records of prayer, Bible reading, self-denial, or heroic service can increase stress and circumvent the benefits of spiritual formation by resurrecting self-centeredness and fueling pride. Thus, even as the ultimate purpose of piano lessons and practice is to make beautiful music, the purpose of spiritual discipline is to break the stranglehold that possessions, people, and self have on us. Albert E. Day clarifies the issue of activity versus achievement: "It is not important how many times you have denied yourself but how truly you have detached yourself from yourself, set yourself free to think of God and love Him."[15] Practice and persistence, necessary as they may be, are only the process. The goal is quality living at its best. Heart wholeness builds on the believer's total commitment to keep the conditions of this requirement from Scripture: "Above all else, guard your heart, for it is the wellspring of life" (Prov. 4:23).

For healthy hearts and satisfying lives, we pray with Dag Hammarskjöld:

Give us
  a pure heart that we may see Thee,
  a humble heart that we may hear Thee,
  a heart of love that we may serve Thee,
  a heart of faith that we may live for Thee.
  Amen.[16]

Exercises to Get Your Soul in Shape

- Begin with conversion.
- Talk to yourself.
- Accept duplicity in others and avoid it in yourself.
- Refurbish your inner world.
- Deal with addictions.
- Turn duty to delight.
- Choose your reactions.
- Start a cheering section.
- Reject spiritual competition.
- Join the Towel Company.
- Renew yourself.

Epilogue

I Love Spirituality

I love spirituality because it exposes my whole life to faith; questions my motives and energizes my will; revolutionizes my affections, so that I love what I once hated; corrects my nearsightedness and tunes the hearing of my soul to the voice of God.

I love spirituality because it warns that possessions can never define my life; shapes my view of the world; shines light into the darkest night of my soul; encourages an accurate modesty about myself.

I love spirituality because it infuses life with a melody, rhythm, and beat; creates a yearning for right living; transforms behavior and makes my faith real and even contagious; refocuses my thoughts about myself, my neighbor, and my God.

I love spirituality because it unites me with serious Christ-seekers in our common hunger for God with the extravagant promise that He will satisfy our souls.

**By no means do I count
myself an expert in all of this,
but I've got my eye on the goal,
where God is beckoning us
onward—to Jesus.
I'm off and running,
and I'm not turning back.**

Philippians 3:13–14

(TM)

Notes

Preface

1. Richard Foster, *Prayers from the Heart* (San Francisco: Harper, 1994), xi.
2. Max Lucado, *The Applause of Heaven* (Dallas: Word, 1990), 10.

Chapter 1: Hunger for the Holy

1. Judith C. Lechman, *The Spirituality of Gentleness* (San Francisco: Harper and Row, 1987), 40.
2. *Newsweek* (June 13, 1994), 31. Albert Schweitzer quoted in Berman, *The Search for Meaning* (New York: Ballantine, 1990), vi.
3. Dag Hammarskjöld, *Markings* (New York: Knopf, 1964), 15.
4. Ted Delaney, "High-tech's High Tool," *Denver Post* (Dec. 8, 1985), G, 1.
5. Michael Dougan, "Success Complicated Life; Wilson Through with Acting," *Colorado Springs Gazette Telegraph* (Sept. 15, 1985).
6. C. S. Lewis, ed., *George MacDonald: An Anthology* (New York: Macmillan, 1986), 34.
7. A. J. Buckingham, "In One Day," *Fort Lauderdale News* (Dec. 23, 1984), G, 1.
8. "November Almanac," *Atlantic* (November 1986), 20.
9. George MacDonald, *Diary of an Old Soul* (Minneapolis: Augsburg, 1975), 52.
10. Quoted in Lechman, *Spirituality of Gentleness,* 55.
11. Richard Lovelace, *Dynamics of Spiritual Life* (Downers Grove, Ill.: InterVarsity Press, 1979), 92.
12. Quoted in Rueben P. Job and Norman Shawchuck, *A Guide to Prayer for Ministers and Other Servants* (Nashville: Upper Room, 1983), 92.
13. T. S. Eliot, *Choices from the Rock: Collected Poems, 1909–1935*, as quoted by Don Postema, *Space for God* (Grand Rapids: Bible Way, 1983), 15.
14. Marilyn Norquest Gustin, *The Inward Journey* (Liguori, Mo.: Liguori Publications, 1991), 67.
15. Jack Canfield and Mark Victor Hansen, *Chicken Soup for the Soul* (Deerfield Beach, Fla.: Health Communications, 1993), 247.

Chapter 2: Cultivate the Center

1. Richard Foster, *Coming Home—A Prayer Journal* (San Francisco: Harper, 1992), np.

2. Stephen R. Covey, *The Divine Center* (Salt Lake City: Bookcraft, 1982), 69.

3. Fulton J. Sheen, *On Being Human* (New York: Image Books, 1983), 312.

4. Thomas R. Kelly, *A Testament of Devotion* (New York: Harper and Brothers, 1941), 115–16.

5. Quoted in Robert Raines, *Creative Brooding* (New York: Macmillan Co., 1966), 112.

6. Thomas R. Kelly, *The Eternal Promise* (London: Hodder and Stoughton, 1966), 48.

7. Mother Teresa, *A Gift from God* (San Francisco: Harper and Row, 1974), 75.

8. George Appleton, ed., *The Oxford Book of Prayer* (London: Oxford University Press, 1985), 7.

9. Calvin Miller, *A Hunger for Meaning* (Downers Grove, Ill.: Inter-Varsity Press, 1984), 40.

10. Vance Havner, *Day by Day* (Grand Rapids: Baker Book House, 1953), 77.

11. Kelly, 23.

12. Frank C. Laubach, *Letters by a Modern Mystic* (Westwood, N.J.: Fleming H. Revell, 1937), 29.

13. Albert E. Day, *Discipline and Discovery* (Nashville: Upper Room, 1977), 100.

14. Kelly, 47.

15. Quoted in R. Huelsman, *Intimacy with Jesus* (Mahwah, N.J.: Paulist Press, 1985), 73.

16. Glenn Clark, *I Will Lift Up My Eyes,* quoted in *A Guide to Prayer for Ministers and Other Servants* (Nashville: The Upper Room, 1983), 93.

Chapter 3: Sing Strength into Your Soul

1. Paul Goodman, *Little Prayers and Finite Experience* (New York: Harper and Row, 1972), 16.

2. James Earl Massey, *Spiritual Disciplines* (Grand Rapids: Francis Asbury Press, 1985), 108.

3. McDonnell, *Through the Year with Thomas Merton,* 163.

4. Kenneth W. Osbeck, *101 Hymn Stories* (Grand Rapids: Kregel Publications, 1982), foreword.

5. Charles M. Sell, *Transitions* (Chicago: Moody Press, 1985), x, xxi.

6. Copyright 1927. Renewal 1955 by A. A. Luther. Assigned to Singspiration, Inc. All rights reserved. Used by permission of Benson Music Group, Inc.

Chapter 4: Pray Change into Your Life

1. Albert E. Day, *An Autobiography of Prayer,* 124.

2. Marjorie J. Thompson, "To Do Justice," *Weavings* (November-December, 1986), 29.

3. Quoted in Halford E. Luccock, *365 Windows* (Nashville: Abingdon Press, 1955), 229.

4. Paul Scherer, *Love Is a Spendthrift*, 101.

5. Quoted in Benson and Benson, *Disciplines for the Inner Life*, 37.

6. Muggeridge, *Confessions,* 67.

7. George Buttrick, *Prayer* (Nashville: Abingdon Press, 1942), 112.

8. Buttrick, 107.

9. Frank C. Laubach, *Prayer, The Mightiest Force in the World* (Westwood, N.J.: Fleming H. Revell Co., 1949), 78.

10. Harry E. Fosdick, *The Meaning of Prayer* (Nashville: Abingdon, 1982), 6.

11. Fosdick, 9.

12. Fosdick, 78.

13. Lawrence, *The Practice of the Presence,* 11.

14. Maxie Dunnam, *The Workbook of Intercessory Prayer* (Nashville: Upper Room, 1979), 22.

15. Calvin Miller, *A Hunger for Meaning* (Downers Grove, Ill.: Inter-Varsity Press, 1984), 75.

16. Horace Walpole, letter to Sir Horace Mann, December 31,1769. Quoted in *The International Thesaurus of Quotations,* ed. Rhoda Tripp (New York: Harper and Row, 1970), 711.

17. Ripple, *Growing Strong in Broken Places,* 165.

18. Richard Foster, *Celebration of Discipline* (San Francisco: Harper and Row, 1978), 90.

19. Steve Harper, *Devotional Life in the Wesleyan Tradition* (Nashville: Upper Room, 1983), 22.

20. Bob Benson, *See You at the House* (Nashville: Generoux, 1986), 95.

Chapter 5: Make Time Your Friend

1. Michael Quoist, *Prayers of Life* (Philadelphia: Westminster Press, 1967), 77.

2. Kenneth L. Gibble, "Listening to My Life: An Interview with Frederick Buechner," *Christianity Today* (Nov. 16, 1983).

3. Milo Arnold, *Adventure of Christian Ministry* (Kansas City: Beacon Hill Press, 1967), 37.

4. Eliot and Breo, *Is It Worth Dying For?* 115.

5. Benson and Benson, *Disciplines for the Inner Life*, 166.

6. Robert Wood, *A Thirty–Day Experiment in Prayer* (Nashville: Upper Room, 1977), 30.

7. Bob Benson, *See You at the House* (Nashville: Generoux, 1986), 53.

8. James C. Fenhagen, *Invitation to Holiness* (San Francisco: Harper and Row, 1985), 57.

9. Quoted in Benson and Benson, *Disciplines for the Inner Life*, 279.
10. Frederick Buechner, *Godric* (New York: Atheneum, 1981), 142.
11. Carstens and Mahedy, *Right Here, Right Now*, 11.
12. Carstens and Mahedy, 12.
13. Francis Fenelon, *Christian Perfection* (Minneapolis: Bethany House, 1976), 29.
14. Frederick Buechner, *Wishful Thinking* (New York: Harper and Row, 1973), 85.
15. Frederick Buechner, *Now and Then* (New York: Harper and Row, 1983), 87.
16. Robert J. Hastings, "The Station," as quoted by Ann Landers.
17. John Henry Jowett, *Yet Another Day* (Westwood, N.J.: Fleming H. Revell, 1905), October 21.
18. Jean de Caussade, *Abandonment*, as quoted by Thomas E. Clarke, S.J., "Never a Dull Moment," *Weavings* 2, no. 3 (May/June 1987):18.
19. Sarah Patton–Boyle, *The Desert Blooms* (Nashville: Abingdon Press, 1983), 43.
20. John W. Gardner, *On Leadership* (New York: Free Press, 1990), 135.

Chapter 6: Follow the Manufacturer's Manual

1. Paul Scherer, *Love Is a Spendthrift*, 79.
2. William Johnston, *Christian Mysticism Today*, as quoted by Benson and Benson, *Disciplines for the Inner Life*, 91.
3. *Newsweek* (Dec. 17, 1982), 45.
4. Frank C. Laubach, *Prayer, The Mightiest Force in the World* (Westwood, N.J.: Fleming H. Revell, 1949), 97.
5. Frederick Buechner, *Now and Then* (New York: Harper & Row, 1983), 9.
6. Terry Hall, *Getting More from Your Bible* (Wheaton: Victor Books, 1984), 42–43.
7. James Z. Nettinga, *Bible Society Record* (January 1968).
8. Hall, *Getting More from Your Bible*, 147.
9. William Barclay, *Fishers of Men* (Philadelphia: Westminster Press, 1966), 17–18.

Chapter 7: Cherish Relationships

1. Vernon Grounds, "Establishing a Faith Fellowship," *Ministries Library Journal* 3:7.
2. John Mogabgab, "Editorial Introduction," *Weavings* 1 (November/December 1986): 2.
3. Albert Schweitzer, *Memories of Childhood and Youth* (New York: Macmillan, 1931), 64.
4. Bob Benson, *See You at the House* (Nashville: Generoux, 1986), 183.

5. Halford E. Luccock, *Treasury of Illustrations* (Nashville: Abingdon, 1962), 14.

6. Oswald Chambers, *Still Higher for His Highest* (Grand Rapids: Zondervan, 1970), 15.

7. Helen Hayes, "Weekend," *USA Today* (Oct. 5, 1986), 17.

8. Peter DeVries, *Forbes* (June 30, 1986), 160.

9. Kathy Coffey, "With Baby and Briefcase," *Denver Post* (Aug. 11, 1985).

10. *Denver Post* (Jan. 27, 1987), G, 4.

11. Grounds, "Establishing a Faith Fellowship," 6.

12. Lawrence J. Crabb, Jr., and Dan B. Allender, *Encouragement, the Key to Caring* (Grand Rapids: Zondervan, 1984), 11.

13. Thomas Merton, *The Wisdom of the Desert* (New York: New Directions, 1960), 71.

14. Ted Engstrom, *The Fine Art of Friendship* (Nashville: Thomas Nelson, 1985), 61.

15. *Colorado Springs Gazette Telegraph* (Aug. 1, 1986).

Chapter 8: Exercises to Make Your Heart Like His

1. Paul Scherer, *Love Is a Spendthrift,* 3.

2. Oswald Chambers, *Still Higher for His Highest* (Grand Rapids: Zondervan, 1970), 18.

3. John W. Gardner, *Self–Renewal* (New York: W. W. Norton and Co., 1981), 13.

4. McDonnell, *Through the Year with Thomas Merton*, 68.

5. McDonnell, *Through the Year with Thomas Merton*, 64.

6. John Kirk, *The Mother of the Wesleys* (London: Jarrold and Sons, 1864), 144.

7. McDonnell, *Through the Year with Thomas Merton,* 153.

8. Rolland Hein, ed., *The World of George MacDonald* (Wheaton: Harold Shaw Publishers, 1978), 44.

9. Eugene H. Peterson, *Praying with the Early Christians* (San Francisco: Harper Collins, 1994), March 9.

10. Sarah Patton-Boyle, *The Desert Blooms* (Nashville: Abingdon, 1983), 166.

11. Albert E. Day, *Discipline and Discovery* (Nashville: Upper Room, 1977), 124.

12. Nouwen, *Intimacy*, 95.

13. Gardner, *On Leadership* (New York: Free Press, 1990), 133.

14. Sheen, *On Being Human*, 315.

15. Day, *Discipline and Discovery,* 131.

16. *Hymns for the Family of God,* 610.